HERMANN HESSE
&
ROMAIN ROLLAND

HERMANN HESSE & ROMAIN ROLLAND

Correspondence, diary entries and reflections, 1915 to 1940

Introduction by
PIERRE GRAPPIN

Translated from the French and German by
M. G. HESSE

OSWALD WOLFF
LONDON

HUMANITIES PRESS
NEW JERSEY

Original French edition
"D'une rive à l'autre" (Cahiers Romain Rolland No.21)

containing parts of the edition by Fretz & Wasmuth, Zurich

Hesse letters and texts

Published by
Oswald Wolff (Publishers) Ltd., London
and
Humanities Press Inc., Atlantic Highlands, N.J.

British Library Cataloguing in Publication Data

Hesse, Hermann
Hermann Hesse and Romain Rolland.
1. Hesse, Hermann – Correspondence.
2. Rolland, Romain – Correspondence.
I. Title II. Rolland, Romain
833'.9'12 PT2617.E85Z/ 78-40861
ISBN U.K. 0-85496-070-8
U.S. 0-391-00913-3

Set by Reproproof Ltd., 7 Soho Square, London W1M 5DD
Made and printed in Great Britain by
Billing & Sons Ltd., Guildford, London and Worcester.

CONTENTS

INTRODUCTION

The dialogue between Romain Rolland and Hermann Hesse began in 1915. A common abhorrence of the war attracted them. On February 26, 1915, Romain Rolland took the initiative of contacting this German writer about whom he obviously knew very little. But he may have known that Hermann Hesse had been living in Switzerland since 1912, a little longer than Romain Rolland himself. And above all he had liked an article in the *Neue Zürcher Zeitung* of November 3, 1914, in which Hesse had evoked Beethoven's music and appealed to the spirit of fraternity, at a time when the din of marching tunes had driven Beethoven's "Hymn to Joy" from peoples' minds. Rolland is surprised and delighted to hear these tones that were so marvellously different. "The voice of Beethoven rescued", he writes in his *Diary*, in which he welcomes Hesse as "one of the best of his race; and he says many things which I could sign".

They first came together through sharing the same sentiments, the same love of music, and devotion to the cause of freedom. During the twenty-five years of their exchange there were to be differences of opinion, as well as disagreements, and more than one disappointment was recorded by Romain Rolland in his *Diary*. But they always found each other again. They are both equally hostile to hypocrisy and conformity. Veneration and silence are preferred by Hesse who often makes a point of saying nothing; brotherly attention is evidenced by Romain Rolland who gives more freely of himself. They came to call each other travelling companions. They both liked long walks, their paths separated, sometimes they lost sight of each other without being too concerned about it, but they followed each other's progress before another brotherly greeting.

During the two World Wars, under the tyrannies and persecutions that embroiled Europe in turmoil and in ruin, they provided an example of friendship and often of lucidity.

As soon as their voices were heard during World War I, they experienced some calumnies. In Germany it was said and written that Hesse had fled from the threat of mobilization even though he had taken up residence in Switzerland some years earlier. Similarly, Rolland was accused of "taking refuge". It is apparent to us, however, though it is more readily seen today than in 1915, that they had chosen an honourable and difficult way. Rolland served here as an example. Hesse gladly recalls it again in his last tribute to his friend in 1956. In the name of a heritage of European culture or on behalf of the artist's universal freedom they had chosen to take their stand on the fine line between withdrawal and solitary courage, between escape from the passage of time and avant-garde action.

In Geneva Rolland worked for the Red Cross, in Berne Hesse concerned himself with the German soldiers who had been wounded or captured and who were interned in Switzerland. Both, but particularly Rolland, found consolation in the understanding letters that came from the trenches rather than from the editing rooms of the capitals after the great war fever of the summer of 1914. Across the fronts and through the intervention of two writers, soldiers of the two nations thus declared their mutual esteem. It was a paradoxical dialogue, but worthy of free men, that was to overcome the heartbreak of having to fire at someone whom one esteems. Succeeding generations – ours – have recognized the madness, both heroic and ruinous for our continent, of this deadly family quarrel, this great duel among Europe's nations. This lucidity has become easy for us, for the past is more easily understood than the present. But in 1915 in Berlin, in Paris, or even in Geneva, very few sensed to what extent the countries of the old Europe were going to destroy each other. On February 26, 1915 Romain Rolland wrote to Hesse:

"We cannot put an end to the madness of the Governments.... It is therefore all the more important for us

to strengthen our bonds – all of us who in all countries repulse with loathing this inhuman insanity and who have the responsibility for maintaining for the future the sacred unity of the European spirit. If the war continues, I believe we must strengthen this purely intellectual union among the free thinkers of all nations." They did it together in 1919 in "The Declaration of the Independence of the Mind".

But there were also discouragement and doubts – especially for Hermann Hesse, the less militant of the two, the more solitary one, the one more apt to seek in renunciation and inner journeying what he despairs of ever finding again in a European humanism. For Hesse this crisis dates back to 1917, the year of bloody and continuous confrontations – from Verdun to the Somme: *"Life here has become difficult, and it has a bitter taste... I do not believe in Europe. I believe only in humanity, only in the realm of the soul here on earth in which all nations participate and whose noblest embodiments we owe to Asia"* (August 4, 1917). That is Hesse's last message to Rolland during the war, except for one article on *Jean-Christophe* in May 1918 in which Hesse reiterates his imagination.

Hesse then forsakes in his mind Europe to seek in the Orient a more humane wisdom, a code more respectful of life, a religion going beyond revelation. This long pilgrimage which is both intellectual and sentimental turns his eyes away from Europe: Hesse does not say a single word about the end of the war in November 1918. Nevertheless he continues to look in Romain Rolland's direction, writes a number of articles about him, and adds his signature to the *Declaration* of 1919. But Hesse understands at the same time how "to spend a new period of solitude, like a recluse in nature."

From Hesse's hermitage there emerges late in 1921 his "Indian" book, *Siddhartha*. This is a book by a follower, not by an observer, of a convert who wants to live what he writes about with manifold joy and at the same time in renunciation. From a distance Romain Rolland followed with understanding Hesse's progress and conversion: *"He has now attained, he maintains, a mentality which fully conforms to his Asian ideals and he creates for himself a life that is in harmony with his thinking. He is completely detached from the entire contemporary world, from art, from today's literature which he regards as a futile game, and especially from politics."* (R.R.'s *Diary*, September 26, 1920), or again later *"India's spirit knocked three or four times at his door before he decided to open his heart to it. He was afraid of being overwhelmed – engulfed. He tells me: Yes, that's so. In India too there's a tiger hidden in the jungle."* Prior to finding a new faith, before attaining a degree of certitude, and in any event before changing his principles, Hesse experienced hesitation, fear and depression: *"He became reassured only when he understood Chinese philosophy and could combine it, as an antidote, with Indian philosophy. Thus he created for himself a personal Asiatism"* (*Diary*, August, 1922).

But Romain Rolland never elected to follow Hesse in his pilgrimage to the East nor to begin a "new life". However, it is evident that his interest in Asia, and especially in India, also grew during these years. Rolland wrote several works on India and very often dealt with it in his *Diary*, and the relationships he had with Gandhi are well known. It is not surprising therefore that he welcomes with joy the fact that *Siddhartha* is dedicated to him and he responds to it enthusiastically: *"What a fascinating vision this torrent of the universe is behind the mask of Buddha's smile! – It continues to absorb me as I come and go throughout the day"* (April 5th, 1923). He asks Hesse also for permission to have *Siddhartha* translated in France. Yet for all that, Rolland does not seem tempted by the adventure of a "new life" into which Hesse had immersed himself without regrets. Because Rolland always felt much closer to the heritage of the Orient and did not believe it necessary to become Indian to understand India and to further Gandhi's cause, he remains in the West.

A short time later, right from the beginning of 1923, began a rather long period of silence in their correspondence, a sign of separation whose reasons were not voiced at that time, at least as far as we know. They waited until 1931 before resuming their dialogue – after seeing each other in Lugano.

However, a letter which Rolland wrote to Paul Amann in 1928 indicates in what direction we should look. Hesse's hermit-like existence, his abandonment of the old rules for the sake of new inspiration, his philosophy that was out of line with this century, his remarks about the pre-eminence of youth, do not always please Romain Rolland. *"No, I haven't been seeing Hermann Hesse for a long time. He always withdraws. I wait for his unstable mood to bring him back to his starting-point. His art becomes always more perfect. In Steppenwolf there are some moving confessions. But basically he is so weak, this false wolf.... I am very much afraid that like the good German he is, he seriously does what our young people merely voice. That was enough, and too much intoxication! If he now uses cocaine!... Our man in his fifties is obsessed by middle age love and even old age love"* (January 26, 1928).

Three years later, however, they found each other again in Lugano, in a harmony that was not to be destroyed, even if their correspondence was to be less frequent: *"Hesse,* Rolland writes, *is much happier and much more balanced than ever before.... He no longer reveals any traces of his past crises. He doesn't deny anything of his earlier philosophy but he harmonizes it with his new life that is without dogma."* (August 26, 1932). When they met in Lugano, there certainly was a discussion, undoubtedly a kind of confession by Hesse. Rolland, who will have heard it as the respected master he never ceased to be for Hesse, has kept it secret and has revealed only its results. The inner anarchy, acknowledged and feared at the same time, which Hesse experienced must have seemed like a danger which was best passed over in silence. We understand why Hesse always spoke of Rolland as someone from whom he received help and comfort. In the prefaces and reviews Hesse continued to write, he always called Rolland a "great consoler", even throughout the years of their separation, and he counted Rolland among those who writings helped him to work.

From 1932 to 1938 the correspondence remains cordial, but infrequent. In some beautiful pages of his Diary Rolland pictures the house of Hesse, the hermit, in Montagnola near

Lugano, an ideal location for an artist *"on the Golden Hill.... with a free view to all sides.... dominating the entire region."* Hesse was to leave it only when he was dying. Rolland, who committed himself more and more to his time, was to leave Switzerland on the eve of World War II, and to return to France, the scene of all the battles, but also of his roots.

In 1933, when Hitler assumed power in Germany, they both experienced sorrow and disappointment. Hesse helps some German political refugees, but experiences above all such heartbreak that he is driven into isolation: *"Once again I had to relive the experiences of 1914. I had to free myself of the sentimentalities and sophisms of patriotism and nevertheless felt like an accomplice of the new attack against humanity and the Spirit."* (Letter written in the Spring of 1933). During the years between 1933 and World War II Romain Rolland often intervened in political struggles, always looking for means of warding off the threats of war. An independent fighter, Rolland remained a kind of "franctireur" – mediating with Stalin against arbitrary imprisonments as well as answering in lofty terms the German authorities whose Goethe prize he refused to accept. However, while Hesse no longer creates, except in contemplative detachment, Rolland, in the midst of the conflict when war, morally-speaking, had already broken out, defends his convictions as a world citizen in every way.

Hesse no longer leaves the heights and perceives only a distant echo of the struggles that perturb the great mass of human beings. In 1938 Hesse felt like an exile in a world that was *"noisier, more mechanized, and more inhuman than ever."* With Hesse, the artist triumphs. The secluded life fulfills an imperative need of his being, in a silence and solitude which he protects, for he is forever susceptible to anguish. Painting in his last refuge, as he is in communion with the elemental emotions of human beings and the joy of colours. Colour, if one considers his painting, appears there like an absolute. It represents the moment when intuition can no longer be troubled by anything and when the artist has the right to be himself completely.

The last word of their correspondence is signed by Romain

Rolland – a quick and friendly card, addressed from Vézelay to Montagnola. It never reached Hesse. The war had been going on for almost a year. France is defeated. It was August 4, 1940. Symbolically the card was stamped on the back "return to sender" – no doubt at the French-Swiss border.

Truly, Romain Rolland was right when he said about Hesse that he was "diametrically opposed to his art". Hesse always sought, both by means he probably inherited from his ancestors and through his Lutheran education, the inner freedom which is the strength and pride of the believer – whereas Rolland, who was committed to the struggles of the outside world, tried not to lose himself in them completely. In this he was as French in his struggle for the good cause as the retreat of Hesse with his passion for the inner life continued the time-honoured tradition of the great Germans. Their correspondence is the dialogue between two artists who want to remain themselves, but who, by doing so, continue also to express a nationality where nationalities harmonize in their love for the universal.

Pierre Grappin

1914

ROMAIN ROLLAND'S DIARY

(November 1914) – ... An excellent article by the German poet and novelist Hermann Hesse in the *Neue Zürcher Zeitung* of November 3, entitled "O Freunde, nicht diese Töne!"* Since he lives in Switzerland Hesse escapes the German contagion. He addresses himself to writers, artists, and thinkers. He regrets seeing them eagerly participating in the war. In expressing his righteous idea, Hesse probably tends to exaggerate the artist's duty to remain silent. This harmonizes only too well with the spirit of German docility. If it doesn't manifest itself in force, it can only conceal its independence within itself. However, I would like to see a thinker from Germany who would resolutely oppose force. Anyway, we have to take men as they are! Hesse is one of the best of his race; and he says many things to which I could subscribe: against writers who arouse hatred; against the humanitarians in peace time who when war breaks out, etc.. Against the war itself, he doesn't want to say anything. He hopes it will be very violent, so that it will end more quickly. And he recommends the attitude of Goethe "who held himself so marvellously aloof during the great war of independence of his people."

* A reference to Schiller's "An die Freude", i.e., "Ode to Joy".

1915

ROMAIN ROLLAND'S DIARY

(18 February 1915) – Hermann Hesse publishes in the *Neue Zürcher Zeitung* (*Abendblatt*) an article on a new German review, *Die Weissen Blätter* of Leipzig, which is reissued after an interruption of several months. Germany's generation of young poets expresses itself in this journal. Hesse calls attention to their great serenity. One of its contributors, the Alsatian Ernst Stadler, has been killed. A lecturer at the Free University in Brussels, translator and friend of French poets, he was supposed to go to Canada last September to teach. He was thirty years old. Hesse compares the journal's Europeanism to mine. He doesn't see in it an isolated exception, but the early flowering of the Europeanism that is latent in the best German youth. Among the most gifted of these young writers, Hesse mentions Werfel, Sternheim, Schickele, Ehrenstein. –

ROMAIN ROLLAND TO HERMANN HESSE

(Agence des Prisonniers de Guerre)

Geneva, February 26, 1915.

Dear Sir,

Your article in the *Neue Zürcher Zeitung* of February 18 has been forwarded to me. I cordially greet you. I wanted to do so long ago –– ever since I read your books, and especially ever since I heard you in the midst of this turmoil reiterate the phrases that dissipate the clouds of hatred –– the words of the exalted Beethoven. We cannot put an end to the madness of the Governments. I fear it will become even more outrageous. And the people cannot speak out. They can hardly think (they are granted neither the time nor the faculty). It is therefore all the more important for us to strengthen our bonds –– all of us who in all countries repulse with loathing this inhuman insanity and who have the responsibility of maintaining for the future the sacred unity of the European spirit. If the war continues I believe we must strengthen this purely intellectual union among the free thinkers of all nations.

Sincerely yours,

Romain Rolland
Beauséjour-Champel Hotel, Geneva

If you are in touch with *Die Weissen Blätter*, please let them know that I would be pleased to read the issue you mentioned.

HERMANN HESSE TO ROMAIN ROLLAND

Berne, Melchenbühlweg 26
28.II.1915.

Dear Mr. Rolland,

Your kind lines were forwarded to me and gave me great pleasure. I reply in German because, although I understand and read French, I don't write it.

I do not know if you are aware that an international journal – a neutral ground for the exchange of ideas and possibilities of understanding among the intellectuals of the warring nations – is to be founded in Switzerland. French contributors are needed. Germans are available. I was offered the editorship of this journal, and it was also hoped that you would be won over. I am a quiet lyricist who lacks the energy for such an endeavour.

The journal is now being prepared by a German-Swiss[1] and a Genevan. I only inform you of it so that you are prepared. The Genevan editor is Mr. G. de Reynold.

I have no personal contacts with *Die Weissen Blätter*. However, I have advised the editor that you would like to see a copy. Many uncouth youths, but also many noble and well-intentioned ones collaborate there.

You know how profoundly I regret the senseless hatred that now separates also the intellectuals in dealing with supranational questions. And yet I firmly believe that the recognition of the necessity of your *union de l'esprit européen* will soon increase enormously. However, for the time being, I refrain from any declaration that may bring politics to mind; for now every well-intentioned acclamation is distorted into something hostile as if it were under an evil spell. The hatred still exists, but it will exhaust itself.

I am glad to know that you are familiar with some of my books. Then you can also imagine how much I like especially the story of Jean Christophe's childhood.

Respectfully yours,

H. Hesse

[1] Professor Paul Haeberlin. (The journal was however never published.)

ROMAIN ROLLAND'S DIARY

(March 1915) – Hermann Hesse sends me his latest poems (which were published in journals): "Frieden", "Der Garten", "Feierliche Abendmusik", "Wandlung".* I find them very beautiful. Through them flows the music and soul of the great old German *lieder*, the profound and simple song of the tranquil soul. – ...

*"Peace", "The Garden", "Solemn Evening Music", "Transformation".

ROMAIN ROLLAND TO HERMANN HESSE

(Agence des Prisonniers de Guerre)

(Geneva), March 10 (1915).

Dear Sir,

Thank you for your kind letter and *Die Weissen Blätter* which were forwarded to me at your request. In the March issue I read several lines of one of your poems*. I would like to read the whole poem. Where was it published? If you'd let me know, I'd be obliged to you.

Sincerely yours

Romain Rolland
Beauséjour-Champel, Geneva.

---

*"O wie klingt der Name Friede jetzt!" ("Oh, How Sounds the Name 'Peace' Now!")

ROMAIN ROLLAND'S DIARY

(April 1915.) – ... A young Englishman, Lionel Wyon, founded in Berne in April an *Europäische Gesellschaft zur Verständigung der Intellektuellen.*[1] The intentions are noble, but extremely vague. I see among its members names that are dear to me, such as Ellen Key, Spitteler, Hermann Hesse. But there are many others who seem questionable to me or barely acceptable. The great majority of them are Germans. I have never had much sympathy for circles of intellectual mobs. But right now I am especially wary of ambiguous societies. I prefer to be a European who fights on alone – independent of every *Gesellschaft.* – ...

---

[1] European Society for Understanding among Intellectuals

HERMANN HESSE TO ROMAIN ROLLAND

Undated

(April, 1915)

Dear Mr. Rolland,

Even when Annette Kolb was here recently, I thought of writing you. Now I have read your Essay in *Le Journal de Genève.* I send you therefore my favourite book as a token of my sincere admiration and with the feeling of spiritual affinity between us.

Yours

Hermann Hesse

ROMAIN ROLLAND TO HERMANN HESSE

Geneva
Beauséjour-Champel,
Wednesday, May 5, 1915.

Dear Hermann Hesse,

What delight your beautiful "music" gave me![1] You are fortunate I am not a composer. I wouldn't be able to resist the temptation to trace a score above your lines. (And poets are never satisfied with it.) You have the genius for the *lied*. What you say is simple and speaks right to one's heart. Your little book has been a dear companion to me every morning in the Champel woods. It was one of many birds –– a bird that sings its nostalgia for the past. Heartfelt thanks,

Yours

Romain Rolland

---

[1] H. Hesse, *Musik des Einsamen.* (*Music of the Lonely Man*).

ROMAIN ROLLAND'S DIARY

(May 1915). ... An invitation from the *Freistudentenschaft** in Zurich to lecture there in June or July with Hermann Hesse (May 2). But I don't accept lectures. – ...

*Society of Free Students

ROMAIN ROLLAND TO HERMANN HESSE

(Bellevue Hotel, Thun)

Monday, August 9, 1915.

Dear Hermann Hesse,

I am your neighbour and would like to see you. Please let me know whether I could come one afternoon this week, about 4.15 p.m.?

Most sincerely yours,

Romain Rolland

HERMANN HESSE TO ROMAIN ROLLAND

Berne, Melchenbühlweg 26

Telephone: 3207

Dear Mr. Rolland,

Forgive me for typing this letter to you. It's due to the fact that I'm in a hurry today. Your kind lines gave me great pleasure. I very much look forward to seeing you, probably Thursday afternoon. I assume you will then stay with us till evening. There's always a plain meal for supper.

Later I will walk with you to accompany you to your train at the Ostermundigen station. It's nicer and closer than the Berne station.

I live rather on the outskirts of the city. In case you don't take a car, please phone me when you arrive, and I'll pick you up at the streetcar stop.

A friend of mine, the German parliamentarian Haussmann will arrive in Thun tomorrow. Haussmann formerly participated in the Franco-German parliamentary conferences and up to the great catastrophe always worked for an alliance with France. I'm advising you of this just in case you should meet him.

Here in Berne the writer Stegemann, known through his strategic articles, is most eager to see you. He is a naturalized Swiss citizen. He thinks impartially and belongs to those who privately do everything to bring about peace.

As far as I am concerned, I would be pleased to introduce you to Haussmann and Stegemann. However I am equally satisfied if you don't desire this and if we are in complete privacy together at my home. I myself am quite apolitical and tend toward an Asian passivity. However wherever I can do anything to promote peace and humanity, I am always very eager to do so. To that end a meeting with those gentlemen could perhaps be valuable. But it's entirely up to you to decide for or against it.

I hope you spend pleasant days in Thun and sincerely look forward to the hour of your visit.

Yours truly

H. Hesse

(Undated letter. Postmark: 10.VIII.1915)

(Bellevue & du Parc Hotels)
(Thun)

Wednesday, August 11, 1915

Dear Hermann Hesse,

I'll come tomorrow, Thursday, around 4.30 p.m. Don't worry about me. After my arrival by train, I'll take a car. I prefer not to meet any politicians for the time being. You probably read my recent letter[1] in the *Int. Rundschau.* For several weeks or several months I'll seek refuge in art. I need it to recover my strength and to find a pure atmosphere once again. I am very sorry that my stay in Thun is now known, for I fear visitors. And I come to inflict my visit on you! – That's human logic ... Until tomorrow therefore.

Sincerely yours

Romain Rolland

I must warn you that while I read German, I don't speak it. Could we talk French? Otherwise our conversation will be quite limited.

[1] Romain Rolland stated in this letter that he would refrain from writing articles on the war.

ROMAIN ROLLAND'S DIARY

(Thursday, August 12, 1915). – I am going to see Hermann Hesse in Berne.

He lives quite a distance from the city, right in the country at Melchenbühlweg 26. It's on the far side of one of the hills that dominate the right bank of the Aar –– closer to the station of Ostermundingen than to Berne's. For three years he has been living in an isolated country house which formerly belonged to his friend, the painter Albert Welti. Hesse lives there with his wife and children —— two rather handsome boys who are eight and ten years old. They spend the whole day like little savages naked from the head to the waist and from the thighs to the sole of their feet, wearing just a plain blue apron around their waist.

Hesse seems about thirty-five years old. He is of medium height. His face is unappealing, his head round. He has very little hair, practically no eyebrows, a thin moustache and blue-grey eyes behind glasses. He appears impassive. He raises his eyebrows when he speaks. His colour is almost brick red. His jaws are strong and emaciated. He speaks French poorly. However he is kind enough to try to speak with me in this language for three hours. (He has not done so, he tells me, for such a long time). This effort certainly accounts in part for the tension of his features. By looking for words and mingling them with some German words, he succeeds in expressing his thoughts very well. His wife —— who is no longer particularly beautiful nor very young, but who looks intelligent and serious —— seems to have a little more facility in speaking French.

At first we sit on a bench at the end of their property. From there one sees in the distance the whole countryside and the peaks of the Oberland Alps spread out before us. Then we sit in his study. The property looks somewhat neglected and the house is old. Hesse works a lot in the garden in summer. He devotes himself to his private life. His study is a beautiful large and wide room, well-lighted, with a comfortable table and several bookcases, filled with books —— many art books and some old editions among them. Hesse is German, but his mother's mother came from Neuchâtel, in the French-speaking area of Switzerland. He is not sure that he won't be recalled to Germany for military service. He hopes not, or hopes to find at least an office job with the Legation in Berne. He is quite determined not to answer if he is drafted. His German patriotism seems most indifferent. Of course he wouldn't like to give up his German nationality for himself. It would seem hardly proper right now. But he considers it for his children's sake. I ask him whether he hasn't sometimes been attacked by the press of his country for his attitude which is somewhat similar to mine (although he is more prudent). He says he has experienced quite a few attacks – but no significant ones. With certain friends, who were once socialists or liberal democrats, but who are now fierce patriots, he says he has fallen out forever. But, he says coldly, he doesn't consider that a bad thing. He adds: *"The fact that we aren't taken seriously exlains why we in Germany don't have to suffer as much from fanatic intolerance as you in France. That's often annoying in peacetime, but it has its advantages in wartime. They say: they are authors behind the times who follow in Goethe's and Herder's footsteps. These names give us some protection. Nevertheless the cosmopolitan is less exceptional, and especially not as new in Germany as in France. He is not liked, but he isn't persecuted."*

Hesse lives quite isolated. His friends in Berne –– there are only a few –– are mostly musicians. One of them, the conductor of an orchestra, set several of Hesse's poems to music. Hesse doesn't play any instrument. His wife, however, plays and, unfortunately, as I learn from our conversation, she is quite conservative in her tastes (which she imparts more or less to her husband). Any new harmony or new rhythm shocks her.

Hesse is particularly visually oriented. He takes a great interest in painting and seems quite well informed about modern artists (Gauguin, Van Gogh). Music always evokes for him images, landscapes. (Thus in a prelude by Cesar Franck –– whom he likes –– he sees high mountains). But he loves nature above all and maintains that it could easily do without all arts (except music perhaps).

Hesse is in contact with quite a few German writers, although he never went to Berlin. He shows more sympathy for Vienna and for the spirit of good-naturedness and affection which dominates that city: this paradise for art where there are so many officers who are artists and writers who are granted a leave to write a novel or an opera (whereas in Germany a civil servant who would be a writer would arouse suspicion). Hesse has become somewhat of a patron of groups of young writers, like *Die Weissen Blätter*. But of these latter he doesn't speak very enthusiastically. Franz Werfel, who is one of those he appreciates most, doesn't seem to Hesse to have much talent. Hesse believes Werfel has reached the height of his literary efforts. He regards him (as I do) too receptive to every new current and superficial. ––– We speak about the enormous –– and ridiculous –– influence of the powerful Walt Whitman (whom Hesse admires as I do) on the young French and German poets. They turn this talented primitive into a dandy; they imitate only his weaknesses and mannerisms and copy his faults. ––– Hesse admires Spitteler, but doesn't like him very much.

For some years now Hesse has been more and more attracted to the philosophy and art of Asia –– at first India's, then China's. Lao-Tse has had a particular impact on Hesse, as he has also on an elite in Germany today. Generally speaking, Hesse admires the Chinese form of thinking and its expression –– this harmonious and quiet ideal that renounces nothing of life, but knows how to calmly enjoy both heaven and earth at the same time –– this perfection of the aristocratic and well-organized life. ––– He has travelled a little in Asia, in Ceylon, Singapore, and Malaya. As he wrote me yesterday, *"Ich bin ganz unpolitisch und hänge einer asiatischen Passivität an."*[1]

---

[1] "I am absolutely apolitical and incline toward an Asian passivity."

HERMANN HESSE TO ROMAIN ROLLAND

My dear Mr. Rolland,

In case it would give you pleasure, I wanted to let you know that the organist of Berne Cathedral is an outstanding expert on German organ music by Bach's predecessors: Buxtehude, Schütz, Moffat, etc. The organist's name is Graf. He is Swiss and speaks French better than I do.

So, if you would ever like to spend an hour with good music, my friend Graf will always be pleased to oblige you. You should just advise either him or me of your visit. (Both of us have a telephone.)

Kind regards,

Yours

H. Hesse

(Undated letter. Postmark: 14.VIII.1915).

ROMAIN ROLLAND TO HERMANN HESSE

(Bellevue & du Parc Hotel, Thun)
(Tuesday, August 17, 1915.)

Dear Hermann Hesse,

Thank you for your charming thought. I'll take advantage of your offer, if I have a free afternoon this week. However, I'll have to go away to Zurich. In any case do thank your friend for me. I do hope to meet him someday.

I was glad I had spent the evening with you. Much more than I, you are rooted in the soil –– like that sheltering tree at your doorstep. You have your house and your family there. I am a restless wanderer whose home has been destroyed. In the course of my travelling, however, I plan to call from time to time on the hospitality of your home for a while.

Kindest regards to Mrs. Hesse.

Most sincerely yours,

Romain Rolland

ROMAIN ROLLAND'S DIARY

...(Between August 17 and August 23.) – On August 14, (1915), Hesse writes me that if I'd like to, his friend Graf, the organist of the *Münster* in Berne, will play for me in the cathedral music by Bach's predecessors – Buxtehude, Schütz, and Moffat – on whom he is an expert.

I can't accept this invitation. (I live in Thun.)...

HERMANN HESSE TO ROMAIN ROLLAND

Dear Mr. Rolland,

It's a pity you didn't come to Berne. But you may still hear the organ music later. Today we drive into the mountains for a few days – for the last time this year and perhaps for a long time to come. From all I hear my age group is soon to be conscripted.

Seeing you again in our home will always be a great joy for me. I wish I could tell you in your own language how dear you are to me and how many of your thoughts affect me like a brother! Oh, this horrible time!

Sincerely yours,

H. Hesse

(Undated letter. Postmark: Berne, 24.VIII.1915.)

ROMAIN ROLLAND TO HERMANN HESSE

(Bellevue and du Parc Hotels, Thun)
Tuesday, August 24, 1915

Dear Hermann Hesse,

I was rather hoping to see you either in Berne or in Thun before my departure. And now I learn from your kind note that you are the one to leave. But I can't believe that you would have to leave Switzerland. (Didn't you tell me that you thought you'd manage to stay, no matter what?) And as I'll continue to live in Switzerland, in Geneva, I expect we'll have the opportunity of seeing each other again. The hours I spent at Melchenbühlweg are a precious memory for me. In my thoughts I'll often see you there. I cordially greet you. ... Just imagine the inhuman law of nations that would have us "enemies"! ...

With very best wishes,

Yours

Romain Rolland

ROMAIN ROLLAND'S DIARY

(October 1915.) – ... Hermann Hesse has sent me his latest work, *Knulp*, three charming tales from Knulp's life. The hero is a likeable rogue, rambler and idler, who wastes his life, is loved by everybody, and who leaves a kind of nostalgia behind him. I understand why Hesse doesn't like Spitteler. One can't imagine a more contrasting ideal. Spitteler lives in the superhuman, the mythical, the colossal. Hesse practices the art of the simple, humane, and harmonious life.

In response to my critical appreciation of *Knulp*, Hesse writes me from Berne. –...

HERMANN HESSE TO ROMAIN ROLLAND

Berne, October 4, 1915.

Dear Mr. Rolland,

Thank you for your generous remarks about *Knulp*,[1] my brother. I haven't been able to write any letter for some time now, because I had too much work and worry. I was drafted at the end of August and I have only now got leave until November 15 because I am engaged in service to prisoners. More particularly, I try to give them reading material, and I plan for them a small weekly paper: that's my favourite idea now. I have just spent a few days in southern Germany, partly for my military leave, partly for the prisoners on whose behalf a new Swiss committee in Berne wants to interest itself. Much love, much passionate work, also much success, but a lot of political and diplomatic opposition. Moreover, in Germany I had the impression that among the people hate is no longer predominant.

– I am enclosing an article herewith.[2] It's a good sign that a Viennese journal, after its initial refusal, nevertheless published it. Terrible news about the war. But perhaps it's really a way to the end! – I was astounded to hear in Stuttgart a *première* of an opera by Schillings: spiritual music, but it isn't a good piece.

– In the garden the leaves are falling. I have hardly time to look out! In the few free hours I have, I read – almost in secret and with a bad conscience – *Don Quixote*.

In your last letter you wrote me: *"Comment pourrons-nous jamais, vous et moi, par quelques forces que ce soit, être constraints de nous haïr?"* * – No, fortunately that's not possible. And love, which conquers death, will one day be stronger and more lasting than today's terror. Once again there will be a Europe, once again there will be a feeling of humanity. You, dear sir, belong to those who have strengthened it in me and in many.

Faithfully yours,

H. Hesse

---

[1] Romain Rolland's letter to Hermann Hesse, to which reference is made here, has not been found.
[2] "Leo Tolstoy and Russia."

*"How could we, you and I, ever be compelled – by whatever forces there may be – to hate each other?"

(December 1915) – Hermann Hesse is insulted by his compatriots, as I am by mine. A newspaper in Cologne,[1] calls him a pacifist and like me, Hesse points out that the feelings of the soldiers differ from those of the journalists who are consumed by hatred. Hesse writes: "This war will have aged me by ten years. But I won't neglect my duty. I won't give the loudmouths a chance. I do hope the time for wrangling will soon be over, and that we will experience a time of working to rebuild on the ruins. This labour ·won't be accomplished by vociferating, gesticulating, or brandishing one's sword. This task will be accomplished through sacrifices. I know that in Germany there are thousands who think like me. And the idle boasting of some angry bureaucrats won't be able to disturb them! I beseech all rational people not to believe that the voice of the bureaucrats is the true voice of Germany." – ...

---

1 Kölner Tageblatt, October 24, 1915.

1916

HERMANN HESSE TO ROMAIN ROLLAND

(Pro Captivis – Berne Bureau Suisse de Secours pour les Prisonniers de Guerre)

(Berne), 9.1.1916.
Melchenbühlweg 26.

Dear Mr. Rolland,

For some months now I haven't had any private life any more. Otherwise I would have thanked you already long ago for your valued book[1] in which I hear again with pleasure your pure and excellent voice. Sincere thanks for this document which is born out of a conviction that one finds today unfortunately among so few! How good it is to know that here and there, there are men for whom it is impossible to commit sins against the spirit!

I, too, have had up to now my share of hostility and slander. Finally I became completely lost in my work. I provide German prisoners with reading material and I had to learn a lot of work which I had never done before. My house has been turned into an office and I don't recognize my garden any more.

My wife extends greetings to you. I wish you above all an effective influence on those who struggle for reason. You have faithful and grateful friends, and these are all the more faithful to you as the number of halfhearted friends you have lost increases.

Respectfully yours,

Hermann Hesse

---

[1] *Au dessus de la Mêlée (Above the Battle)*

HERMANN HESSE TO ROMAIN ROLLAND

Berne, 22.1.1916.

Dear Mr. Rolland,

I recommend to you (not to be polite, but with sincerity) Dr. Wyss. She has for a long time devoted her activities, which I esteem highly, to soldiers and prisoners. Please receive this lady's suggestions and plans just as if they came from me!

Faithfully yours,

Hermann Hesse

ROMAIN ROLLAND TO CHARLES BAUDOUIN

Geneva, January 23, 1916

... Those isolated from Germany can hardly be reached any more. They have been drafted these last months – or, having been threatened, they are silent. However, here is the address of one of the best: *Hermann Hesse, Melchenbühlweg 26, Berne.* But this poet (one of the foremost of the young Germany) has been severely attacked by the Pan-German press. Since then he has become all the more prudent because he has been drafted. – ...

ROMAIN ROLLAND'S DIARY

(2nd week of July 1916.) – ... On the boat from Thun to Gunten – where I'm going one afternoon with my family[1] – I meet Hermann Hesse. His face is thin and lined. He tells me he has experienced much mental anguish since last year. He lost his father. He has seen too many oppressing things. This winter he has been suffering from "neurosis". He finally got permission to stay in Switzerland. He has been drafted. But he is engaged in the service for prisoners of war, and especially in library work for the internees. He wants to occupy them to prevent them from becoming neurasthenic. He organizes courses for them in Berne and various other cities. He goes to Gunten to interest a rich German lady in this work. – Hesse estimates at 3000 the number of German internees in Switzerland. Among them is Moïssi, the famous actor, with whom I concerned myself recently at Wilhelm Herzog's request. As his friends had asked, Moïssi, who was an aviator and prisoner, has been sent to Switzerland, to Arosa, as a TB patient. He is quite ill, but is enthusiastic about the war. (Undoubtedly this results from his illness.) His only wish is to be sent back to the front. He says that he saw some terrible things, but it gives one such a sense of exaltation that once one has had a taste of it, one can never forget it. – Hesse knows of few writers who have been victimized by the war. According to Hesse, the best was Trakl. On the other hand he knows of many talented painters. – Hesse is in a strange situation. His father, a German Russian, came to Switzerland. Hermann Hesse and one of his sisters are German, a brother and another sister are Swiss. – He has great difficulty speaking French and speaks it very poorly. Like Schiller conversing with Mme de Staël with great seriousness, Hesse searches slowly and calmly for his words (he rarely finds the exact ones) and follows the train of his thoughts without worrying about ridicule. – ...

---

[1] From time to time Romain Rolland's family joined him in Switzerland.

(October 1916.) – ... Professor Fr. W. Foerster just came from Zurich to see me. Foerster doesn't like the professional pacifist. He speaks of Alfred H. Fried with a certain (polite) disdain and considers him superficial. He expresses himself with even greater (but still courteous) irony regarding

Hermann Hesse whom he finds too gentle, somewhat dull, and lacking energy. According to Foerster the pacifists make the mistake of forgetting too much the real conditions of humanity. He says: *"I believe that there really is in humanity an original sin"*. He means the warring and fighting instinct. One must take it into account and reckon with it, if one intends to fight it effectively. – ...

1917

HERMANN HESSE: 'JEAN CHRISTOPHE IN PARIS[1]

Delayed by the war for more than two years, the second volume of *Jean-Christophe* has finally appeared in German. This translation by Erna and Otto Grautoff is published by Rütten und Loening in Frankfurt.

This volume should have appeared earlier. But even now it will be welcomed by thousands of readers: that is the way it should be, and we have fulfilled our debt of gratitude.

There is no belligerent country whose people hate us as much as the French, whereas it is precisely towards this country that our interests and our sympathies are directed. Every Frenchman who isn't absorbed by militant hatred is of infinite value for us, and of this small number the best and the noblest is Romain Rolland.

His work is doubly welcome here in Germany – both insofar as it is a literary masterpiece and insofar as it is a book that, already before the war, valiantly criticized France.

Not every page of this book is poetry; many pages are artificial, although of very good quality. Zeal, conviction, and courage manifest themselves on every page. – And besides the France which Rolland judges with so much *sang-froid* and which we have also known, the reader discovers in this very rich book many things about a France which we have known too little and which, after the war, must matter to us – this France where, apart from fashion and great success in the arts and sciences, the dignity and the integrity of convictions are still honoured.

We respect and honour Romain Rolland inasmuch as he is representative of this aspect of France.

May Rolland – through the sufferings of the war which has also brought him personally much anguish and many insults – not lose courage, and may he preserve the necessary energy to accomplish his mission!

---

[1] Text published in the review *März*, June 30, 1917.

ROMAIN ROLLAND'S DIARY

(July 1917) – ... In *März* (Stuttgart, June 30) is a short and very sincere article by Hermann Hesse about *Jean-Christophe in Paris,* which has just been published in German.

On the same book there is in the *Journal de Zürich* a very *sympathetic* article entitled "Der Bürger Europas"*.

---

* "the Citizen of Europe"

ROMAIN ROLLAND TO HERMANN HESSE

Saturday, July 18, 1917.

Dear Hermann Hesse,

Forgive me for failing to thank you earlier for your very cordial article on *Jean-Christophe in Paris.* You know, I'm sure, how greatly I value your judgment and your understanding.

I do hope you feel better than on the occasion of our last meeting on Lake Thun. I think of you with loyal affection. Kindly convey my respects to Mrs. Hesse.

Affectionately yours,

Romain Rolland

Hotel Byron, Villeneuve (Vaud)

HERMANN HESSE TO ROMAIN ROLLAND

Berne, August 4, 1917

Dear Mr. Rolland,

Your kind greetings gave me sincere pleasure. Since then I have been ill and very lonely. Life here has become difficult, and it has a bitter taste. Whenever possible I turn away from the contemporary to the timeless. Poetry, therefore, has become ever dearer to me. I have failed in my attempt to devote myself to political things. Also, "Europe" doesn't represent an ideal for me – as long as men kill each other, under Europe's leadership, I suspect every classification of people. I do not believe in Europe. I believe only in humanity, only in the realm of the soul here on earth in which all nations participate and whose noblest embodiments we owe to Asia.

Dear Mr. Rolland, you belong to the few human beings whose name represents for me hope and merit.

Sincerely yours,

Hermann Hesse

ROMAIN ROLLAND'S DIARY

(August 1917.) – ... Hermann Hesse, whom I had thanked for his short article in the *März* review, answers me with a melancholy letter. He is completely disenchanted with Europe and seeks refuge in the reveries of Asian art and philosophy. (Berne, August 4.) – ...

ROMAIN ROLLAND'S DIARY

(November 1917.) – ... Almost simultaneous visits from Stefan Zweig and Mrs. Cruppi. – ... He (Zweig) cautions me

(I didn't need to be warned) against almost all German writers who are in Switzerland. There are hardly any who are not more or less in collusion with their government. This is the case with Schickele and the members of his review who are considered heroes of civic courage in Germany. Zweig says: "I know what to think of that kind of courage." Among the German writers who are in Switzerland he makes hardly any exceptions – except for Hermann Hesse whom he likes very much. (Zweig just met Hesse in Berne and likes him very much, as well as Fritz von Unruh.) – ...

1918

ROMAIN ROLLAND'S DIARY

(April 1918) – ... Stefan Zweig, who returns from the *Congrès International des Femmes pour la Paix** held in Berne, writes to me. (20 April)

– ... (I had told him how I was prevented from reaching my parents. They have been held up for two weeks in Savoy, without any means of forwarding me a message or of seeing me from a distance at the border. Twice I returned in vain to Saint-Gingolph. I didn't see them again ...).

Zweig writes that Hermann Hesse had to endure even more: "... *His father had died. He wanted to go to the funeral to see him once more. And he had to wait, wait in the passport offices, while his whole being was consumed by solemn grief. He recounted this tragedy he experienced*"** –...

* International Women's Congress for Peace

** "Zum Gedächtnis"

HERMANN HESSE: "JEAN-CHRISTOPHE"

Romain Rolland's novel *Jean-Christophe*, which was published in the original French edition in ten volumes, is now complete in the German edition. (It has been translated by Otto and Erna Grautoff and published by Rütten und Loening, Frankfurt, in three large volumes). The last volume, *Journey's End,** has just been published.

When such voluminous works are involved, it frequently happens that their beginning captivates us, but that the work as a whole does not remain on the same height. Of course, *Jean-Christophe*, too, is very uneven indeed in its quality. From the artistic or poetic point of view I consider the first part – the story of Jean Christophe's childhood and adolescence – the most notable. But be that as it may, there will not be a reader who does not like the work as a whole. There will not be any reader who, apart from the passion and intuition of the successful parts, does not admire also the patience and the labour, the intelligence and the spirit of justice in the other chapters.

Now a work like this is not pure literature. It is more and it is less. From the point of view of pure art, a beautiful lyrical poem of four lines is more perfect and has greater value than any novel, including *Wilhelm Meister*. – A novel like *Jean-Christophe* is not only a work of art. It doesn't express only the vitality of a soul. This novel is also the attempt of a mind to judge intellectually, and to a certain extent with a sense of collective justice, the image of a period, of a culture, of a part of humanity. The musician Jean-Christophe is not only a representative person or a creator's original vision. He is at the same time an entity that has many meanings – almost a myth. Jean Christophe is the soul of music, the spirit of German genius, unrefined and awkward for whom Paris – gracious and attractive, depraved and childish, mad and splendid – is a mirror, a stimulus an excitement, a paradisical attraction that becomes indispensable for him: there lies his destiny.

Romain Rolland, who is French, has portrayed his German hero with greater sympathy than he has for the unknown Paris. For a thousand pages our solicitous compassion goes out to the musician who struggles against the cruel, false, and blind Paris. On the surface this is so everywhere. Everywhere Parisian morals, manners and ill manners are implacably criticized, while Christophe always enjoys the same sympathy. It would seem that Christophe is right and that Paris is wrong.

In reality this is not so at all, and one of the main attractions of the book is that the external, cruel, and corrupted Paris is the object of a sacred and profound love. Paris is raised to a height that is much greater than any love and any critique could ever assign to it. It is an impassive and powerful reality and becomes a destiny of anyone who comes into contact with it. – The French and particularly those of the war time, still do not realize what Song of Songs has been sung in this book to the glory of their Saint of Saints. Up to the war many Frenchmen believed Romain Rolland was an author who made a virtue out of his little weaknesses for Germany. In Germany he was similarly judged. In reality Rolland is profoundly French – a true representative of the French *esprit*.

And that is precisely why it is doubly meaningful and invaluable that this same Romain Rolland belongs to the small number of those for whom, even in wartime, love for mankind and generally recognized international values remain something serious.

This man has not only written books of an exceptionally good quality and intelligence. Not only has he refused to participate, in exchange for some petty laurels, in public shouting and incitement to hatred, he also –without glorifying himself – handed the Nobel Prize which was awarded to him over to the International Red Cross in Geneva. But to remain true to himself, he also renounced his glory, his friendships, the treasure of his fatherland and of love which he had reaped.

The time will come when the courage of this type of man and actions which appear passive today, will show it's vitality. Then it will be realized that Romain Rolland's conduct was more Christian than one might think. And in his great musical novel not only his critical intelligence and his great ability will be admired, but also his passionate love for justice, this love that is full of respect and good will for everything that is truly human.

---

[1] Article published in the *Vossische Zeitung*, Berlin, May 1918.
**(La fin de Jean-Christophe, Johann Christof am Ziel)*

ROMAIN ROLLAND TO HERMANN HESSE

Thursday, July 25, 1918.

Dear Hermann Hesse,

A young Japanese friend, Seichi Narusé, has come to see me. (He is here now.) We have been corresponding for several years. He translated my *Vie de Tolstoy.** He is very congenial and intelligent. He admires you and would like to see you very much. Will you be in Berne next week? He intends to go there, mainly to meet you there. He'll probably return to France, within the next eight to ten days, and from there go on to Japan.

Affectionately yours,

Romain Rolland

Byron Hotel, Villeneuve (Vaud.)

**Life of Tolstoy.*

ROMAIN ROLLAND'S DIARY

(August 1918.) ––– ... My young friend Seichi Narusé leaves Villeneuve on August 4th after having spent a fortnight here. We devoted every evening to long conversations. He goes to Berne for a day or two to meet Hermann Hesse there. –––...

1919

HERMANN HESSE TO ROMAIN ROLLAND

(Croix-Rouge Suisse – Division Pro Captivis
Secours aux Prisonniers de Guerre
Rédaction du Sonntagsbote)

Berne, January 24, 1919.

Dear Mr. Rolland,

Will Vesper, a German poet, sends me the enclosed Appeal with the earnest entreaty to publicize it everywhere wherever possible. I am sending it therefore also to you. Unfortunately everything he says is absolutely true.

Aggrieved, but as always, affectionately yours,

Hermann Hesse

WILL VESPER'S APPEAL[1]

Since I don't know if there are still men —– I mean adults —– who are not poisoned by hatred and the lies of war, I address myself to you, the children of the whole world. And I beseech you to listen to me for a moment! Do you know that while you play and amuse yourselves, there are millions of children who have been suffering hunger for many years now and who are to suffer hunger even longer. Every morning they get a few thin slices of bread, of poor, black bread, because we have no longer any yeast – and every mouthful they eat that day is rationed for them – miserable food without milk, and without meat and practically without any fat. Moreover, even this food is severely restricted. – It must be rationed for them so that the next day an equally miserable mouthful may be between them and death. And every evening before going to bed they come to their mothers who have even less than they to eat and say: "Mother, we are so hungry! Mother, we could still eat so much more!" – If that keeps up for three days, it may seem like a joke. But if this continues for three months, it means heartache. If it lasts for three years, it means despair and often results in death. People are now sent to us who want to see if it's true that we are dying of starvation. – However, they mustn't go into hotels where the rich and those who don't have any children to feed can still get many things for a lot of money. Let these people go to the families and look at our children who were once energetic and healthy like you, but who have become pale and sick. Just think about it: To be starving by degrees every day for three years! How cruel and terrible that must be!

Germany is a poor country and too small for the size of its population. It doesn't produce even half of what it needs for its people to exist on. Germany has always bought its food from other richer countries. In those countries there is now also enough food. But the countries that are waging war with Germany have blocked this food so that it no longer reaches Germany. So many terrible things have happened everywhere in the course of this war. But that was the most evil of the weapons employed to win the war, which drained Germany of its strength and took its courage away. And the worst is that whereas all other arms have long ago been put down, this invisible cannon continues to bombard our children every day, and kills them every day by means that are even worse than the previous ones. We speak of humanity, of justice, and of brotherhood among the nations. We want to believe in them from the bottom of our hearts and because of our faith we have laid down our arms. But look, so far we have heard only words, words with which one cannot still the hunger of even a dog, while our children are dying of starvation.

The President of the United States of America came to Europe to act, as we firmly believe, on behalf of humanity and the ideals he proclaimed. But does he know that since he has been in Europe humanity has not progressed but has regressed? Does he know that after having surrendered all railway coaches, locomotives, machines, and tools that were demanded of us, we can no longer really provide bread for our children? Are these children meant to be killed? If it's the intention to decimate us Germans, then let this bloody vengeance be carried out openly and quickly. Destroy us according to the old war law which was really kinder! Let one out of every ten Germans be executed! But then – in Christ's name – if His name still has any meaning at all somewhere – give our children food.

I beseech all greathearted and freethinking men to disseminate this Appeal as soon as possible!

Will Vesper[2]

---

[1] "To the Children of the Whole World", to aid Germany's starving children.
[2] Romain Rolland immediately forwarded this text to Mrs. Louise Bodin, writer, feminist, and pacifist.

ROMAIN ROLLAND TO HERMANN HESSE

Tuesday, April 29, 1919.

Dear Hermann Hesse,

With my latest published book[1], I forward you a copy of the *"Déclaration d'indépendance de l'esprit"*[2] which I recently drew up in agreement with Georg Fr. Nicolai and which has already been approved by a few free European intellectuals (Bertrand Russell, Benedetto Croce, Frederik van Eeden, Stefan Zweig, Barbusse, etc.). Are you in agreement with it? And if you are, would you do me the favour of adding your name to ours? I'll only ask you not to discuss it before we have received the most important replies expected and until we are ready to publish our Appeal. I hope you and your loved ones are in good health.

Always yours affectionately,

Romain Rolland

Villeneuve (Vaud), Byron Hotel.

---

[1] Colas Breugnon
[2] "Declaration of the Independence of the Mind"

DECLARATION OF THE INDEPENDENCE OF THE MIND

Intellectual workers, comrades scattered throughout the world, separated for the past five years by arms, censorship, and the hatred of nations at war, now that the barriers have been let down and the frontiers have been reopened, we address an Appeal to you to form once again our fraternal union – a new union closer and stronger than the one that existed before.

The war threw our ranks into confusion. Most intellectuals placed their knowledge, their art, their reason in the service of their governments. We do not intend to accuse or reproach anyone. We understand the weaknesses of individuals and the elemental strength of great collective forces: the latter overwhelmed the former in no time at all because nothing had been anticipated to resist them. May this experience be a lesson to us, at least for the future!

First, let us note the calamities which resulted from the almost total abdication of the world's intelligentsia and its voluntary subservience to the forces that had been unleashed. The thinkers and artists have added an immeasurable amount of poisoning hatred to the scourge destroying Europe's body and mind. In the arsenal of their wisdom, memory, and imagination, they sought old and new reasons, historical, scientific, logical, and poetic reasons for hating. They worked to destroy mutual understanding among men. And in doing this, they disfigured, reduced, depreciated, and degraded the Idea whose representatives they were. They made it (perhaps without realizing it) the instrument of the passions and egotistical interests of a political or social clan, of a State, of a fatherland, or of a class. And now when all nations concerned – be they victorious or conquered – come bruised out of this barbarous conflict, they are ashamed and humiliated in their heart of hearts (although they don't admit it to themselves) by the madness which seized them. And the Idea, compromised by their conflicts, emerges debased with them.

Arise! Let us free the Mind from these compromises, these humiliating alliances, this hidden subservience! The Mind is the servant of no man. We are the Mind's servants. We have no other master. We are created to carry and to defend its light, to rally around it all men who are lost. Our rôle, our duty is to maintain a fixed point, to show the pole star amidst the storm of passions in the darkness. Among these passions of pride and mutual destructions, we do not single out any one, we reject them all. We commit ourselves never to serve anything but the free Truth that has no frontiers and no limits and is without prejudice against races or castes. Of course, we do not dissociate ourselves from Humanity. We toil for it – but for all Humanity. We do not recognize peoples – we acknowledge the People – unique and universal – the People who suffer, who struggle, who fall and rise again, and who always advance along the rugged road that is drenched with their sweat and their blood. We recognize the People among all men who are all equally our brothers. And so that they may become, like us, ever more conscious of this brotherhood, we raise above their blind struggles the Arch of Alliance – the free Mind that is one, manifold, eternal.

HERMANN HESSE TO ROMAIN ROLLAND

Address after May 10:
Montagnola near Lugano

May 2, 1919.

Dear Mr. Rolland,

How much pleasure your greetings and gift gave me! The bottle of old Burgundy[1] will console me as soon as I find in Montagnola another home after having been without one for a long time.

Today I don't have the peace of mind to write to you properly. But I want to express at once at least my unreserved approval of your admirable *"Déclaration d'Indépendance de l'Esprit."* (sic) Please add my name to it as well.

In my personal life I have lately had to bear a heavy burden! Just now I am about to spend once more a short time in the Tessin as a hermit to enjoy nature and to earn a living with my work.

I think of you very often with the sincerest approval and respect.

Faithfully yours,

Hermann Hesse

---

[1] Hesse refers to the book *Colas Breugnon* which Rolland had sent him.

ROMAIN ROLLAND'S DIARY

(Paris, 4 June 1919.) . . . Jane Addams gives me her agreement. And I learn from Jouve that Werner von Heidenstam and Hermann Hesse also sent me theirs to Switzerland. – . . .

HERMANN HESSE: SOME BOOKS[1]

. . . To conclude, yet another foreign book – a French work. In any case the work of a Frenchman who, although he is also an architect of today's mentality in France hasn't devoted a single hour of his life to militant hatred. He is Romain Rolland. His *Colas Breugnon* comes as a beautiful and happy surprise. It is not a book about current problems. There is nothing tragic and no dream for the future in it. But it is an entertaining book, full of sunshine and wind, a rural atmosphere and morning freshness, and of old, sweet wine – a book as good and cheerful as good health itself. To no one more than to this man, to Rolland more than any other, we must be grateful for belonging to a small group of supernational humanitarians. Yet in the fifth year of the war he still had to undergo very bitter experiences in his own country and did not have the right to treat himself to such carefree pastimes. I add frankly that in spite of my great love and the great respect I have for this courageous hero, I have been embarrassed for some years by Rolland's commitment to current and polemical problems. I would have liked to hear a song by him, his expression of the simple joy of living and the portrayal of a humanity without problems. Gradually Rolland became a Servant of Humanity, but was he still a poet? Was he still childlike enough? Was he still naïve enough for pure inventions, for the pure and primitive joys of creation? Here is the answer – the finest answer he could give[2]. In the copy of the book he sent me, Rolland wrote a short dedication, which is the most appropriate remark that may be made about this book: *"Ce flacon de vieux bourgogne, pour tenir tête à la mélancolie."*[3]

---

1 Article published in the *Neue Zürcher Zeitung*, July 13, 1919.

2 H. Hesse did not know that *Colas Breugnon* had been written before the war.

3 "This bottle of old Burgundy against melancholy."

HERMANN HESSE: ON THE NEW FRENCH LITERATURE[1]

Some of Romain Rolland's works have been published in Germany by Rütten und Loening, Frankfurt. The most recent work to appear is his *Michelangelo*.

In his *Die weissen Blätter*, Schickele has accomplished much in developing exchanges between the French spirit and the German spirit. May we find again the ways to the old European spirit of which French literature is the classic expression, or may this spirit impel us still further towards liberation and a renaissance. – The doors must be opened. Exchanges and communications between us and foreign countries, free intellectual intercourse must again become possible and normal throughout Europe. Even in the spring of 1919, just when Romain Rolland had to suffer personally from the fanatic nationalism of his own country, he launched – with intellectual representatives from all European countries – an Appeal whose aim was to renew intellectual intercourse. And even in the summer of 1919 there were in Germany still newspapers which got upset and severely reproached those Germans who signed the Appeal.

Do we want to continue in this spirit until Germany has been destroyed again, or do we prefer to relinquish this spirit to Clemenceau and his followers?

---

[1] Article published in *Vivos Voco*, October 1919.

1920

HERMANN HESSE: ROMAIN ROLLAND'S MICHELANGELO [1]

Rolland's *Michelangelo*, just like his *Beethoven* and his *Tolstoy* (which, by the way, will also soon be published in Germany), is not a dull, educational book, in contrast with other such works. The author of this book does not aim to make people understand what the expert knows about Michelangelo by retracing the steps of his difficulties. Instead his aim is to educate through the example of a great man. The best French literature of the last twenty years has been educational. It has an ethical background and Romain Rolland ranks foremost in it. In his *Michelangelo,*[2] whose excellent German edition is embellished with a dozen reproductions by Michelangelo, Rolland stresses the human side. Rolland attempts to elucidate Michelangelo's painful process of accepting his destiny and to interpret the soul of this solitary artist. In spite of his great historical knowledge, Rolland always follows closely the leading thread, instead of concentrating on a description of the Renaissance period, as is usually done. For the small group of "intellectuals" (a horrible word!) who during the war conscientiously struggled against hatred among nations and fought for the defence of reason, Romain Rolland was a born leader. He will continue to be a leader for many of those who are now awakening, as the misery and gloom of the war years end, and who seek to build on the ruins of their faith in humanity.

---

1 Article published in *Bücherwurm* V, May 1920.
2 Published by Rütten und Loening.

(September 1920.) – . . . I just found by chance in the *Kalender für Schweizervolk: O mein Heimatland!*, 1918 (edited by Gustav Grunau) an article by Hermann Hesse: "Erinnerungen an Indien" which comments on some truly beautiful sketches of Chinese and Malaysians by Hans Sturzenegger of Schaffhausen. This Sturzenegger was Hermann Hesse's travelling companion in the Far East, and Hesse recalls their common recollections. They left in the summer of 1911 and without interruption made the passage from Genoa to the "Straits Settlements". One splendid evening in Penang they were suddenly caught up in the boisterous life of an Asiatic town. Hesse recalls briefly some of his most striking impressions: *"The pensive walk of a Hindu, the gentle and sadly beautiful fawn-like expression of the delicate Sengalese, the stark whites of the eyes of the dark and bronze-coloured Tamalian coolie, the smile of an aristocratic Chinese..."*. And further on: *"Proud and self-possessed the Mohammedan of India, dignified and serene the calmly walking Chinese, timid and graceful the small slender Ceylonese, skilful and obliging the handsome Malayan, small and intelligent the industrious Japanese."* Hesse is conscious of the humanity common to all these races and his own . . .

ROMAIN ROLLAND TO HERMANN HESSE

Lugano, Victoria-au-Lac Hotel
Friday, September 24, 1920

Dear Hermann Hesse,

Carl Seelig told me that you are still living near Lugano. If you come here some day, I would be very happy to see you. I would go myself to Montagnola, were I not such a poor walker since an attack of 'flu last year. It would be advisable, if you come, to drop me a line the day before, because I may have gone out. And it would be even better if you could come to lunch with me at the Hotel. I'll certainly be here for another fortnight at least – with my sister. I hope you are well.

Affectionately yours,

Romain Rolland

ROMAIN ROLLAND'S DIARY

(September 1920) – . . . Hermann Hesse, who has been living for the past two years in Montagnola, above Lugano, comes to dinner (September 26). He is thin, gaunt, clean-shaven, ascetic, severely cut to the bone – like a figure by Hodler. Hesse has gone through an exceptionally severe crisis from which he has emerged – according to him – as a new man. External circumstances have contributed to it – his wife is mentally ill and confined to a hospital; he is reduced to poverty, his children are separated from him and are in schools in northern Switzerland. Hesse lives in complete isolation, and his material existence is reduced to the minimum. Under these circumstances the old principles, implanted in his mind by India and China, which had always attracted him, have developed in an exceptional manner. He maintains he has now attained a state of mind which fully conforms to his Asian ideals and he creates for himself a life that is in harmony with his thinking. He is completely detached from the entire contemporary world, from art, from today's literature which he regards as a futile game, and especially from politics. He is even detached from almost everything that gives value to life for the modern man: comfort and public esteem. Hesse lives like a wise man from India (even though his ideal is rather the wisdom of China with its cheerful accommodation to life). Hesse claims he is happy. To keep busy and to earn some money, he has taken up painting. He embellishes with sketches the manuscripts of his poems which some collectors buy. Last year he published a work under a pseudonym.[1] No one knew his secret. Hesse says it was the first manifestation in him of a new-born man. The work made its impact itself on account of its own merits, and the real name of the author ultimately became known. But Hesse is absolutely intent on this proud self-denial of his public personality and is determined to keep his private life free, separate, and hidden from the public. The origin of Hesse's development goes back to a trip of five or six months which Hesse once made to the Far East, to Singapore, Sumatra, etc. In contrast to Nicolai, Hesse was, from the very first days, irresistibly attracted to Chinese life – even though he saw only its humblest representatives. But it seems almost as if precisely these interested him most – the coolies, the yellow rabble. Hesse speaks with affection and envy of their smile for everyone, of their capacity for happiness despite the misery they must bear. – Hesse tells me about the amazing attraction that Asian philosophy holds for modern Germany. The main initiator of this movement has been Count Keyserling with his *Reisebuch eines Philosophen*[2] which contains many superficial pages, but also some very fine ones. Keyserling, whose mind is exceptionally subtle and accomplished, espouses by turns the philosophy of Asia which he encounters along the way and that of Europe when he returns to the Old Continent. Keyserling has founded in Germany a school to teach the Hindu methods of ecstatic concentration. – Hesse says what he writes now appeals to the sympathies of a part of German youth, but that all his former friends break away from him because they fear the actual influence of his works. Although Hesse repudiates absolutely all political action, he himself acknowledges that his thought can (unconsciously) be exploited by present-day passions – in a Bolshevist sense. And that's the nightmare of his old public, made up of "liberals" (i.e., they are today apprehensive conservatives). However, Hesse adds, I am convinced that striving for personal liberation, according to the way Asia interprets it, is the only thing with which we can oppose Bolshevism. But the masses can't manage it. And Bolshevism will thrive no less through them. – To be sure! he says, in an indifferent tone – ...

---

[1] *Demian*

[2] *A Philosopher's Travel Diary.*

(October or November 1920.) – . . . I am on an outing with my sister to Montagnola where Hesse has his home. It's not at all a retreat lost in solitude, as I had expected. Montagnola is one of the cleanest and prettiest villages in the vicinity of Lugano – on the crest of the hills which dominate at one and the same time the three branches of the lake – that of Lugano to Castagnola, Gandria, S. Mamette; that of Agno; and that of Ponte-Tresa. The countryside is enchanting and varied: vineyards, meadows, chestnut trees, fig trees, pomegranate trees; green slopes, undulating lines of mountains studded with villages. Pleasant little houses (we look at a country-house that is for rent, in perfectly good order); a good little hotel which is moderately priced. And there seems to be a small colony of German writers and artists who come, like Hesse, to seek refuge here against the hardships of our time. (There is postal service by car three times a day, from Lugano.) – . . .

1921

HERMANN HESSE: STEFAN ZWEIG'S ROMAIN ROLLAND[1]

The first German biography of Romain Rolland has been written by Stefan Zweig. He has known the French writer for a long time and during the last years of the war often found himself near him, and even at that time he declared himself openly for Rolland's pacifist ideal. – This biography appears now at the right moment. Even if it is not yet possible to make a completely valid judgment about Rolland the writer, Stefan Zweig has expressed in his excellent book the enduring qualities of Rolland's intellectual character and what he means for our time. Zweig's work has grown out of a sympathy and respect whose passion burns in many moving and fascinating pages. I can share this act of faith: for me, too, the figure of Rolland has been, during the war years, a consolation and a guarantee of the permanence of European thought. The testimony, the approval, and even simply the presence alone of this solitary and courageous witness gave me also, on certain days of despair, during those fateful years, the possibility of spiritual survival. For many it has been the same. Rolland's life and private destiny throughout the war have aimed to occupy this solitary position and to exercise in spite of that his influence everywhere at the same time. Zweig's book demonstrates this convincingly.

---

[1] Article published in *Wissen und Leben*, Zürich, 1921.

ROMAIN ROLLAND TO HERMANN HESSE

Villeneuve (Vaud),
Villa Olga,
Monday, November 7, 1921

Dear Hermann Hesse,

I have just rented a little house in Villeneuve where from now on I'll spend a part of every year – for the sake of my work as much as for my health, which has been rather poor these past months. I intend to return to Paris – towards the end of this month and will stay there until April. Then I'll return here. – I hope you are well. I have heard recently of a certain fine project of a hand press which you and Mardersteig handle. – Allow me to ask you for some information. Could you indicate to me the translations and German editions which have been published of Chinese philosophers, and especially of Lao-Tse? I would like to acquire them. Do you know *Wu Wei,* a work of fiction based on the philosophy of Lao-Tse, by the Dutchman Henri Borel? (The French translation was published by Fischbacher in 1912). It seems like a very fantastical work to me.

I hope to see you soon.

Affectionately,
Your friend,

Romain Rolland

HERMANN HESSE TO ROMAIN ROLLAND

Montagnola, Nov. 8, 1921.

Dear Romain Rolland,

Thank you for your greetings from Villeneuve. I am delighted that you now have a permanent home in Switzerland, and I wish with all my heart that this stay will also be beneficial to your health.

I am sending you along with this letter a little snatch of a poem that is dedicated to you. I couldn't send it to you earlier since I didn't have your address. Please accept it in friendship.

And now I come to your questions:

That Mardersteig and I handle a hand press, or something similar, is a legend whose source I can't explain. What is true is merely that Mardersteig, one of the directors of the Kurt Wolff Publishing House, often stays here in Montagnola – but not because of me. I come in contact with him only very seldom.

However, it is true that I publish a kind of publication of which you have perhaps heard – but I do so without any publicity. Enclosed is a prospectus as a curio.

And now I come to Lao-Tse. For many years he has been for me what is most consoling, as far as I know. The word Tao represents for me the quintessence of all wisdom. Several translations of this little book are available – a poetic one, freely transposed by Ular; another one by Klabund, even more poetic but absolutely free, terribly free, terribly removed from the original; and some other translations. I can recommend only two good translations which are as close to the original as possible: Richard Wilhelm's translation (published by E. Diederichs in Jena) and Julius Grill's translation (published by T.C.B. Mohr in Tübingen). I prefer Wilhelm's translation.

For more than ten years now a collection of Chinese thinkers in German translation has been coming out under the Diederichs imprint in Jena. This collection is edited by this same Richard Wilhelm and up to now I can recommend it highly. *The Conversations of Lao-Tse, Lia-Dsi, Confucius, Oschuang Dsi* (Tschuang Tse), *Mong Dsi* (Mencius) – translated in their entirety by Wilhelm – have already been published. Richard Wilhelm has spent many years in China. I know a lot about him through one of my cousins who spent fourteen years in Japan as a professor and with whom I am on very intimate terms.

About myself – I have nothing important to tell you. I have a few problems right now. My hopes for the immediate future are that I can maintain, if possible, my Swiss refuge where I can work and find peace again. Otherwise I'll take up my travels once more. All my attempts to find somewhere in Switzerland an employment which would allow me to earn a living have been unsuccessful.

My dear friend, I do hope we will meet again in Switzerland. In case you come here again one day, you'll find me still in the same circumstances. I live like a recluse in Montagnola, but my marriage has not yet been dissolved. One of my children still lives with his mother, and the other with friends.

This Tessinian autumn is wonderful. Until the day before yesterday, I only needed one fire in the grate. The days were like crystals – blue and clear; and the garden is still full of roses.

Most sincerely yours,

Hermann Hesse

SIDDHARTHA.

An Indian Story by Hermann Hesse

*(*The First – and so far only – *Part)*[1]

To Romain Rolland

Dear and revered Romain Rolland,

Ever since the autumn of 1914, when somewhat earlier the persecutions against the Mind had abruptly begun to reach me too and we believed in the same international truths – ever since then I had intended to present you one day with a token of my affection which would be at the same time an example of my work and which would give you an insight into the essence of my thoughts.

Please accept in friendship the dedication of Part I of my Indian composition which is still incomplete.

Hermann Hesse

[1] Published in *Die neue Rundschau*, XXXII. Jahrgang der *Freien Bühne*, Band 2, S. Fischer Verlag, Berlin und Leipzig.

ROMAIN ROLLAND TO HERMANN HESSE

Villeneuve, Villa Olga
Tuesday, Nov. 22, 1921.

Dear Hermann Hesse,

My health accounts for the fact that I haven't answered your letter earlier. I was delighted with your Hindu story, and I am most touched that you dedicated it to me. What? If I hadn't written to you, I might have been ignorant for a long time of both the work and the kind words prefacing it? Do quickly note my two addresses: in Paris, 3, rue Boissonade (XIVe) – I'll return to Paris at the end of next week – and in Villeneuve, Villa Olga, where I intend to spend next Spring and Summer.

Siddhartha ends at a most important moment, namely when you must expound your own thoughts. I look forward to the continuation with great interest.

Thank you for your information on the German translations of Chinese philosophers.

Have you never been in touch with Tagore with regard to the Asian University he wants to establish in Bolpur? – I don't know how you feel about Tagore? Perhaps you consider him too European, or perhaps his art seems to you altogether devoid of insipidity. – I must say I was somewhat prejudiced against him, especially when I saw the snobbery surrounding him. But I had the great pleasure of seeing him privately in Paris last Spring. I have become deeply attached to him and have a profound respect for him. He is highly intelligent and has an acute understanding; he is by no means taken in by people. And now in his independence in the midst of numerous difficulties which arise from his admirers as well as from his enemies, he suffers intensely under the European brutality which he hates. He radiates an astonishing harmony that has grown out of his rich experiences and anguish. – Tagore is keenly interested in having some Europeans come to his University, and I would consider it for later on, if my health were not too impaired now. But Tagore comes up against so many obstacles – put up by his compatriots as much as by the English!

Most affectionately yours,

Romain Rolland

1922

HERMANN HESSE: TOLSTOY'S LIFE [1]

Anyone who knows something about Romain Rolland's life knows also what an important rôle Tolstoy played in Rolland's life. Rolland was a young student in Paris when one day, being tormented by scruples of conscience and hesitating between an artistic vocation and an ethical vocation, he addressed a letter to Tolstoy to which he certainly expected no answer – for it was more of a confession and an attempt to see himself clearly rather than a profession of faith, and more of an appeal for help than a question. And then this amazing thing happened. The old Russian who is celebrated throughout the whole world sends to a young Parisian student a letter full of sympathy, understanding and consolations – a very long letter.

This incident has been of enduring importance in Romain Rolland's life. And when about ten years ago he wrote his biography *Tolstoy* [2] which only now appears in German, it was not simply a book, it was not simply a good literary study. It was also the expression of a profound gratitude, a great love and veneration that lasted a whole lifetime. That Rolland could write such a book on Tolstoy – so human, so affectionate and so alive a book – must be attributed to the influence of that letter he had earlier received from Tostoy. For this letter had then shown him, the young Rolland, that Tolstoy was not only a great artist and an influential preacher, but also a man of great benevolence and fraternal sentiments. Rolland's book on Tolstoy concentrates particularly on this – on Tolstoy the man, on the unending and painful struggle of his difficult and righteous life, having experienced many difficulties and disillusionments, many disappointments and torturing scruples.

Nevertheless, this infinitely beautiful book is not a simple biography. It deals in depth with Tolstoy's works and the literary influence of his works, especially his first books: *The Cossacks, War and Peace,* and *Anna Karenina.*

The pages where Rolland comments on *War and Peace* are indicative of what is most beautiful in Rolland's work. As one reads Rolland's book it is a joy to see what a sympathetic attitude can accomplish. It is a rare and extraordinary pleasure to learn how this Frenchman has understood this Russian; how this man of culture, artist and connoisseur has understood the naïve and disturbing critic of art; how this European with a socialist bent has understood this eastern mystic; how he has done him justice. It is a delight to see how Rolland has nowhere insisted on the doctrines, and how he pursues, detects and exposes even in the excessive outbursts of Tolstoy's iconoclastic temperament, not the faults and isolated expressions, but the inner life. While he clearly expresses his preference for Tolstoy's early literary works, Romain Rolland nevertheless also refrains from leaning toward the current conception which considers the works about religion and ethics as an aberration, as a regrettable activity of a genius who has gone astray. Romain Rolland courageously opposes this superficial idea which is still quite widespread here. Rolland also manages with loving sympathy to do justice to Tolstoy's last works. It is true that in his analysis of *Resurrection* Rolland, it seems to me, insists too little on the artistic error which consists in the fact that the hero Nekliudov fulfills a mission which his character does not allow him to take on. Particularly with regard to this characterization, I would have liked to see a more thorough analysis of Tolstoy's complex psychology and a reference to the duality which forced the writer to attribute to his hero his own ideas and the most personal problems he had experienced. – Yet he had represented his hero too little after his own image. Even in his earliest works, Tolstoy sketches his own image here and there. In a rather timid manner he half exposes and half hides himself. Nevertheless he tends to put into the mouth of his own characters his personal profession of faith. This tendency to confess to a faith, while fleeing from time to time from it, is no mere game for Tolstoy, but a key to Tolstoy's whole psychology, however abnormal and eccentric it may appear to be.

It is not a lack of understanding, but rather his affection and respect, which prevented Rolland, not only from alluding to the profound suffering in Tolstoy's life, but also from explaining it. Rolland indicates on one important page how little Tolstoy's intense need for love, even the commandment "Love thy neighbour as thyself" satisfied him because this commandment left him with an impression of egoism. But that is precisely Tolstoy's problem: Tolstoy's problem is not one of his mind and of his art, but lies rather in the distressing dilemma of his personal life. Only rarely and with difficulty did he find within himself a true love for himself, while he fulfilled more easily the duty of loving his neighbour, even if this demanded sacrifices and suffering.

I wanted to say here only that I miss something in Rolland's book. This is not a criticism, for it would be absolutely impossible for me to criticize this magnificent book. I simply express an idea which came to my mind. As far as the rest of Rolland's book is concerned, I could not express anything except joy and gratitude and the wish that it will be widely distributed. The problems with which Tolstoy struggled are, in part, no longer the problems of today. But they are immortal and could at any moment and for any man become once again burning issues.

---

[1] Published in the *Frankfurter Zeitung*, February 28, 1922.
[2] *Vie de Tolstoy*

HERMANN HESSE: PIERRE ET LUCE[1]

A Novelette by Romain Rolland[2]

Among Rolland's great works, the short and charming *Pierre et Luce* might be eclipsed. But it contains some pages of the purest poetry. It is the story of a couple of lovers – an eighteen-year-old high school boy from Paris and a poor little girl who has to work to earn a living. Both are still almost children, but over both broods a threatening destiny as the war is raging outside Paris.

Pierre has already been earmarked for conscription and has only a few weeks or even a few days left. Just as some beautiful and gentle flowers which belong to another world blossom in the midst of exploding grenades and among the dying, these two graceful children grow in their love in the midst of a Paris at war.

---

[1] Text published in *National Zeitung*, Basel, June 22, 1922.
[2] German edition published by Kurt Wolff, Munich.

ROMAIN ROLLAND TO HERMANN HESSE

Villeneuve (Vaud) Villa Olga,
Monday, August 7, 1922

Dear Hermann Hesse,

Are you in Lugano? From August 18 to September 2 International Conferences will be held there to which Duhamel, Frederik van Eeden, Count Kessler, Bertrand Russell, and various others, will come – among them some very interesting Hindus, my friends Kalidas Nag, a history professor at the University of Calcutta, and Dilip K. Roy, an expert on old Hindu music. Perhaps you would be interested to go there. We would be very happy to see you there. From the attached programme you will see that these conferences were to be held in Varèse. But at the last moment the violence of the Fascists who are in power in Varèse, as in Milan, made the meeting in Italy impossible. Thus it was decided to transfer it to Lugano. A telegram received today informs me that the Meister Hotel has just been rented for this purpose. – Except for the meeting-place itself, nothing has been changed as far as the terms indicated on the prospectus are concerned.

– If you need further information, please write to the *General Secretary, Miss Emily Balch, 6 rue du Vieux Collège, Geneva.*

I hope you are in good health and satisfied with your work.

Affectionate greetings.

Most sincerely yours,

Romain Rolland

These conferences are not of a political nature. They are meetings of free intellectuals.

It is sincerely hoped that Chiesa will agree to take part. – I don't have his address.

HERMANN HESSE TO ROMAIN ROLLAND

Montagnola, August 10, 1922

Dear Mr. Rolland,

Your kind letter opens with the question whether I'm still "in Lugano". It's difficult to respond to that question. I'll answer by saying that I still live in Montagnola, but I haven't been in Lugano for more than a year, although it takes only about an hour to get there. You'll understand from this what kind of a life I'm leading: St. Jerome in his study.

Thank you very much for your announcement. If the Conference does take place, I'll try to attend parts of it and I would be very pleased to meet your Indian friends.

After almost three years my *Siddhartha* is now just about completed. This winter it will be published in book form. You'll receive it then immediately. The first part of the book is still dedicated to you. I dedicated the second part to one of my cousins who has been living in Japan for some decades. He is fully conversant with the philosophies of the East and we are particularly close.

I am pleased to know you are again in Switzerland. And I hope we'll meet again some day.

Some months ago I lost a dear friend, Konrad Haussmann, the German politician. Germany's intellectual atmosphere has a somewhat anarchical, yet also a religious-fanatical, character. It's a state of mind which resembles that of the end of a world and the advent of a millennium.

Sincerest greetings and best wishes.

Respectfully yours,

Hermann Hesse

HERMANN HESSE TO ROMAIN ROLLAND

Montagnola, August 25, 1922.

Dear Mr. Rolland,

I must reiterate my thanks for your last letter. Quite frankly, at first I was apprehensive about the League's intrusion into my retreat. And I agreed to give a lecture only reluctantly. Instead of giving a talk, I read the conclusion of my *Siddhartha.* Only few could understand *Siddhartha.* Mr. Kalidas Nag understood it all the better. He quickly became a dear friend for me and I want to thank you especially for his acquaintance. Twice I spent several hours with him, in the company of an interpreter. An affinity of opinions that I have found only very seldom revealed itself.

Your sister invited me for dinner on Monday. Mr. Nag will also be there. As every day we'll be thinking of you with affection.

I also found understanding for my kind of thinking on Duhamel's part – at least, as far as the language allowed. We hope that through his intervention it will be possible to publish one of my more recent books in French in Paris. However it would seem even more important to me that an English edition of *Siddhartha* be made available. (The

German edition will be published in a few months.) This book would be for many English readers and also some Asian readers a sign that supranational and timeless thoughts unite us.

Greeting you with renewed feelings of kinship and affection,

Most sincerely yours,

Hermann Hesse

ROMAIN ROLLAND'S DIARY

. . . (August – September 1922) – . . . International Conferences (organized by the Ligue Internationale des Femmes pour la Paix et la Liberté,* August 18-September 2).

– . . . In spite of the chaos caused by the necessity of transferring the seat of the Congress from Varèse to Lugano, a fortnight before its opening, the Congress was a success. The Tessin extended a warm welcome to the many members (125) of the Congress who felt sincerely congenial.

– . . . Duhamel opens the series of conferences with a talk on 'Individualisme et Internationalisme'** – "clearly individualistic and directed against the masses", my sister notes.

Frederik van Eeden has great success with his 'Conseils à la jeunesse'*** which he had submitted to me first. His sincerity was so obvious that even those most removed from his religious tendencies were touched.

Van Eeden met Hermann Hesse and at once "they became spiritual brothers. They spent a day together in Montagnola in the mystic regions of philosophy." But Kalidas Nag especially was "impressed by the exceptional intuition with which Hesse penetrated and assimilated the philosophy of the Orient. This seems to Kalidas Nag unique in Europe".

– Hesse reads in public a part of *Siddhartha,* his new work.

– Most interesting is the evening I spend with Hermann Hesse who comes from Montagnola to dine with us and

Kalidas Nag. Hesse had not left his retreat for a year. He went to the Congress – not without apprehension – only at my request. He is glad, however, he met Kalidas there, and he thanks me for it. Hesse is strangely ugly – (my sister refers to "the appearance of a Buddhist monk") – but he makes an immediate positive impression because of his inner strength and perfect simplicity, his sincerity and truthfulness without the least compromise. While he speaks French poorly and with difficulty, he is not afraid of speaking slowly and choosing the right words. And what he says is never unimportant. He attributes to his ancestors his astonishing attraction to the Indian mentality. His maternal grandfather, who travelled there, knew four Indian languages. Hesse's mother spent her youth there. He himself made only a short trip there. But he says India's spirit knocked three or four times at his door before he decided to open his heart to it. He was afraid of being overwhelmed – engulfed. (At one point I tell him the news from Bounine where one evening a European – suddenly panic-stricken – can't stay another night in India and flees. And I see how Hesse's eyes shine. "Yes, that's so In India too there's a tiger hidden in the jungle.") Hesse became reassured only when he understood Chinese philosophy and could combine it, as an antidote, with Indian philosophy. Thus he created for himself a personal Asiatism. – But I realize what agony and suppressed turmoil are masked by this wisdom from Asia – this ascetic and serene discipline which Hesse imposed upon himself and which he has been manifesting with nobility for some years. This ravaged face, scarred by ordeals, is transfigured by the impressive tranquility of a strong will. But with its anguish hidden, this will knows its own limitations and apprehends everything that might reveal them to its inner enemy. When I was about to leave a radiant Hesse says to me: "This has been our finest meeting." I reply, "I can't forget our first meeting in 1915 when we saw each other and found we were friends in the midst of war." – "Yes", he answers. "It was beautiful. But then there was war and now there is peace." – "I have no illusions and no disillusions", I respond. "For me, at that time the war wasn't much more and now it isn't much less. The war goes on."

Hesse becomes melancholy. "No", he says. "I must believe that the war is over. I must be optimistic because I have a tendency for dejection" (that's not the word he uses, but his gesture is much more expressive.) "I couldn't stand my work for the prisoners of war a second time." – Kalidas Nag, who discusses it with me the day after, is very much struck by this anguish which is controlled, but which always lies underneath this firm foundation of Buddhist-Confucianist wisdom. – Hesse shows us some remarkable aquarelles he painted himself. Now he enjoys painting as much as writing poems; and for him painting complements writing. In his last paintings there is something that reminds one of Douanier Rousseau. Hesse's style, however, is more moderate and even. – I buy one of Hesse's books, *Wanderung,* which he has embellished with some first-rate landscapes.

---

* International Women's League for Peace and Freedom
** Individualism and Internationalism
*** Advice to Youth

ROMAIN ROLLAND TO ROGER AVERMAETE

Villeneuve,
Sunday, September 3, 1922

. . . – I arrive from Lugano where I was present for the final days of the International Conferences – really very interesting. A lot of people – speakers and students – from every country. (This time even the French came). A very lively and congenial atmosphere. Especially a series of conferences and discussions on Asia which were quite outstanding. Some Hindus and Japanese; and Bertrand Russell gave an account of the year he just spent in China. And Félicien Challaye spoke about (Khmer) art and ruins in Angkor which he visited twice, at an interval of twenty years, before and after the big excavation works. Let me not forget the exceptional personality of Hermann Hesse, the German poet, who has penetrated the Asiatic philosophy so profoundly that the Hindus were lost in astonishment that a European could assimilate their spirit so completely. – . . .

ROMAIN ROLLAND TO HERMANN HESSE

Villeneuve (Vaud), Villa Olga
Wednesday, September 13, 1922.

Dear Hermann Hesse,

I acquired your charming and musical *Wanderung*. But I would like to know where the aquarelles have been published. I saw only very briefly a collection of them that was printed in your name. Please oblige me by asking your publisher to forward me this collection, billing me. The earlier the better for I would like to show it to guests whom I expect.

I was very glad to see you again. I found you stronger and calmer, more sustained by your wisdom – perhaps happier? – At least that was my impression. I always judge less the spoken words than the radiance that emanates from every one.

Frederik van Eeden wrote to me again to say how happy he was to have met you. He has taken you to his heart.

My sister sends her best regards.

Affectionately,

Your friend,

Romain Rolland

HERMANN HESSE TO ROMAIN ROLLAND

Montagnola, Sept. 15, 22.

Dear Romain Rolland,

Thank you for your kind letter.

Since you need the album of aquarelles[1] urgently, I'm

sending you one directly. If you want it, you can forward me 12 francs. I'm adding for you a small aquarelle which I'd like to dedicate to you.

I'm in poor health, but in good spirits. Our meeting in Lugano remains a beautiful memory and an inspiration for me. Our Indian friend has also already written to me.

Should you come again to Lugano, I'll do my utmost to receive you here in Montagnola as well. In my retreat, here, among books and pictures, in a crowded study high above all trees, is my own atmosphere which is really an integral part of me – as it should be for a truly wise man. Kalidas Nag thought that everything here in my cell reminded him of India.

Thinking of you often and rejoicing in your existence,

Most sincerely yours,

H. Hesse

---

[1] *Elf Aquarelle aus dem Tessin,* Recht-Verlag, Munich (Eleven Aquarelles from the Tessin)

ROMAIN ROLLAND TO HERMANN HESSE

Villeneuve,
Monday, September 18, 1922.

Dear Hermann Hesse,

I am delighted with your album of aquarelles. They are delectable like fruit, and cheerful like flowers. They are a heart's delight. We like them very much! Thank you for sending them to me and for having added the original aquarelle, which I treasure.

Of course I look forward to seeing you one day in your retreat above the trees. It's unfortunate that poor health prevented me from visiting you last week.

Affectionate greetings,

Yours Romain Rolland

I am forwarding you a money order for 12 fr.

HERMANN HESSE TO ROMAIN ROLLAND

Montagnola, September 23, 1922.

Dear Romain Rolland,

Since your kind letter indicates that you like such things, I'd like to show you something herewith. From time to time I make such a booklet for a friend. This one is a new fairy tale[1] in which the text and the pictures are not to be separated.

The booklet is intended for a friend of mine and has just been finished. Please return it to me in a few days, but you don't need to rush yourself particularly.

You see from this work even better than from the other portfolio what my efforts at painting represent and how painting and poetry are interdependent for me.

It's likely that I'll have to travel in October to take a cure. Right now we have perfectly golden Autumn days.

Most sincerely yours,

Hermann Hesse

---

[1] Hermann Hesse refers to the manuscript of *Piktors Verwandlungen* (Piktor's Transformations) and the accompanying drawings.

ROMAIN ROLLAND TO HERMANN HESSE

Wednesday, September 27, 1922.

My dear Friend,

Thank you very much for having sent me your charming little book. (I am returning it to you, simultaneously, by registered mail.)

The story is exquisite – and very evocative. (You are really not very demanding, my friend Hesse, when you restrict your desires to being a tree with two heads – with that of your beloved! *Beata solitudo!* – You are an epicure of the retreat. I ask for nothing better than a cell which is as well occupied. – But I don't expect it from this world.)

The illustrations are amusing. Nevertheless I admit I much prefer your landscapes. Undoubtedly that's because humour can be transmitted less easily than poetry from one race to another.

I'm studying right now with Gabriel Belot a system of illustrations which is an integral part of one of my books.[1] I envisage particularly some drawings in the wide margin and some ornamental sketches that unfold themselves around the text like a border of plants and grotesque sketches that are interspersed throughout the text.

I like the wreath of flowers and the knot of vipers at the beginning and end of your book very much.

Sincerely Yours,

Romain Rolland

---

[1] *Colas Breugnon*

If you happen to come this way, I expect you to visit us without ceremony for lunch or dinner. Don't forget that we – my sister and I – value our friendship with you.

HERMANN HESSE: **CLERAMBAULT** *BY ROMAIN ROLLAND* [1]

In a perfect translation by Stefan Zweig, Romain Rolland's *Clerambault* has also just been published in German.[2] Together with his articles which appeared in *Le Journal de Genève* during the war, *Clerambault* is the strongest, the most thoughtful and the most personal profession of faith against the war, against the lack of spirituality and heartlessness of our nations, of our politics, and of our press. Rolland could say that he wrote this book – more than any other – with his blood. May this *Histoire d'une conscience libre pendant la guerre** – whose original title was *L'Un contre Tous*** and whose contents were experienced between 1914 and 1918 by some of us in our own hearts – also be cordially received in Germany.

---

[1] Text published in *Vivos Voco,* III, October 1922.
[2] Rütten und Loening, Frankfurt.
* *Story of a Free Conscience During the War*
** *One Against All.*

HERMANN HESSE TO ROMAIN ROLLAND

Kurhaus Degersheim
(Saint-Gallen)

Dear Romain Rolland,

For the past three weeks I have been here for a very exhausting cure and I still have to stay here for another fortnight.

I'm sending you today an article[1] which may give you some pleasure. Then please forward this article to Kalidas Nag if you have his address.

Here we already have snow and for three weeks we had dense fog. I am fasting, perspiring, and doing gymnastics. I still weigh 108 pounds.

I expect to return to Montagnola no later than early in December.

Heartfelt greetings to you and your sister,

Yours

H. Hesse

(Undated letter. Postmark: 8.XI.1922)

---

[1] "Besuch aus Indien" (Visit from India.)

ROMAIN ROLLAND TO HERMANN HESSE

Villeneuve, November 11, 1922.

My dear Friend,

Thank you for your letter and the journal. But just now I can't find them and the information on your present address. So I must send this letter to you in Montagnola.

Kalidas Nag's address in Paris is: 17, rue du Sommerand, Ve. I just received a letter from him.

The young poet Paul Neubauer (from Nové Mesto in Czechoslovakia) has asked me to kindly introduce him to you. He is sending you his first volume of poetry, *Wohin?* * which has just been published by Tal. I couldn't judge its literary value in a language I don't master perfectly. However, his personality is ardent and sincere.

I hope your stay in the mountains will have renewed your strength completely.

Sending you affectionate greetings,

Your friend,

Romain Rolland

---

* *Where?*

1923

ROMAIN ROLLAND'S DIARY

(Early in April 1923) – . . . Hermann Hesse's *Siddhartha,* whose first part is dedicated to me, is one of the most profound works a European has ever written on (and in the spirit of) Hindu philosophy. When he read it in Lugano, Kalidas Nag was filled with admiration for *Siddhartha.* The last fifteen to twenty pages may be added to the treasure of Hindu wisdom. They don't merely paraphrase it, they complete it. Hesse writes me that none of his other works has been greeted with such absolute silence. His friends haven't even taken the trouble to thank him for it. – . . .

ROMAIN ROLLAND TO HERMANN HESSE

Villeneuve,
Thursday, April 5, 1923

My dear Friend,

I feel guilty for not having written to you earlier about *Siddhartha.* But for such a book I couldn't offer you just the usual polite thanks. I had to meditate. I regret the delay.

How beautiful and profound the conclusion of the work is! What a fascinating vision this torrent of the universe is behind the mask of a Buddha's smile – of a *Vollendete!** It continues to absorb me as I come and go throughout the day. But I thought: How many – among today's writers – can understand it except for its picturesque aspect? My friend Hesse, how many see in your work – beyond the disguise of the novel, the literary attire – the OM** that your soul sings like the river? Even among those who are close to you, who admire and love you – how many suspect your true self? You would certainly find more in India than in Europe. Our friend Nag must translate this book into Bengali.

I should also like to urge Bazalgette to ask your permission to have it translated into French for the collection he edits in Paris. But will the good Parisians be mature enough to appreciate the hallucinating beauty of such a work?

I am moved by it and I am glad that its brilliance should come at such a time from the Golden Hill and from a wise friend who is dear to me.

Affectionately yours,

Romain Rolland

---

* Perfect one
** "The Perfect One" or "Perfection"

Kind regards also from my sister.

Who published your book *Aus Indien*?* And does *Aufzeichnungen* mean simply "Notes" or are also actual drawings in the book?

---

* *From India*

HERMANN HESSE TO ROMAIN ROLLAND

Montagnola,
April 6, 1923.

My Dear Friend Rolland,

For no other book yet have my personal friends forsaken me as they have done for *Siddhartha.* Almost no one even took the trouble to drop me a line to acknowledge its receipt. Your dear, beautiful letter which I received this morning pleased me all the more!

You are right. Among my colleagues extremely few can appreciate and understand *Siddhartha.* From public critics I have heard so far only expressions of respectful bewilderment.

On the other hand there are a few people for whom *Siddhartha* is completely straightforward, accessible and dear – both with regard to its Indian and its human qualities and with regard to my quite personal mythology. These people take it in as if it were the atmosphere of their homeland. The best among them is the one who shares with you the dedication of the book – my cousin in Japan. He has learnt quite a lot, having spent more than fifteen years in East Asia and having had long and intimate contacts with Japanese *bonzes.**

Thank you therefore for your kind consideration of my book. And thank you also for the idea of recommending it in Paris for a French edition. I would welcome this very much. The less this book means to the masses, the more I am interested in having it made accessible here and there to the few individuals who are of significance for me. This would require both a French and an English edition.

Your question about my book *Aus Indien*** embarrasses me a little. Well, I'll tell you all about it. In this work there is a short story from the Anglo-Indian world which pleased me very much then (1911) and which I regard even now as a good story. But unfortunately the major part of the book's contents – notes of my earlier journey to Malaya, Sumatra and Ceylon – doesn't deserve a recommendation. The book is shallow, and the trip itself was really a disappointment – that is at the time, because later it bore most beautiful fruit. But then, at a time when I had fled to India because I was weary of Europe, I found there nothing but the excitement of the exotic. During the trip itself this physical exoticism did not bring me closer to, but alienated me rather from, the Indian mind which was familiar to me even then and for which I was searching.

Now, with *Siddhartha* I have been able to pay off a part of my debt to India, and I believe I'll probably never again need the Eastern disguise.

Our friend Kalidas hasn't written to me for a long time. I

fear that my last letter to him dating back about two months must have been lost.

We have a marvellous Spring and I try to paint again the small trees with their beautiful blossoms that I like so much. But this time I find everything difficult, for I am not in good health. I am in great pain and I can walk only with difficulty. However, the doctor promises me a cure in Baden. I'm now trying to make arrangements for this treatment and, if I succeed, I hope to go there in May.

How fortunate we poets are after all. He who tries to express as a poet his relationship to the world that is so greatly diversified and stratified has so many better and more fitting means than the person who expresses himself in a purely intellectual manner. This can be seen especially clearly today with Count Keyserling whose noble and significant intellectuality becomes very banal because of the way he expresses himself. This is also true of Tagore's journalistic essays. Nevertheless Keyserling and Spengler, both of whom I have been reading lately, have become very dear to me. Both of them display this exaggeration and arrogance which is common in Germany among its scholars and especially among the younger ones. They regard the existence of their colleagues as competition and imagine that the New Era starts with them. But all this is merely a front. Behind it lies in both cases an outstanding substantial nucleus from which much can be gained.

Please extend sincerest greetings to your dear sister! I am counting on it that both of you will be longing again sometime for Lugano, and that you will then also come and see me sometime in Lugano. In Lugano I really don't feel at home. I feel there almost as much a stranger as in Berlin. But up here in my study, with its simple quietude and rusticity, which has nevertheless all the refinements of an epicure's retreat – only here do I really and fully live.

Sincerest greetings, my dear and honoured friend,

Yours,

Hermann Hesse

---

* Buddhist monks
** *From India*

HERMANN HESSE TO ROMAIN ROLLAND

Basel,
Krafft Hotel,
December 7, 1923.

Dear Romain Rolland,

For a long time I've wanted to send you one of my aquarelles. Today I'm finally going to do it. It's a Tessinian study from Montagnola. But I'm sending it to you from Basel, for I've been here for some weeks so that I can spend – for the first time in five years – the winter in the city. However, I can no longer take an interest in most of the city's attractions. What I appreciate most is my well-heated room and the masseur who treats my sciatica. But from time to time I also listen to music. Tomorrow, for example, I'll hear Haydn's "Creation" and I look forward to it. However here too I can't find my way back to socializing, not even through my forthcoming marriage in the near future.

At heart I am a Samana* and I belong to the forest.

Cordial greetings,

Yours,

Hermann Hesse

---

* Ascetic

ROMAIN ROLLAND TO HERMANN HESSE

Villeneuve, Villa Olga,
Tuesday, December 11, 1923.

Dear Hermann Hesse,

How much joy you give us! Your aquarelle is charming. It brightens up our room these grey winter days. It's like music. I'm afraid that since you have such a liking for painting, you'll gradually turn away from ink and words.

I am sending you my little volume on Gandhi[1] which appears simultaneously in French in Paris. Andrews and Pearson, the Mahatma's companions, whom I saw this year, provided me with much information on him.

Our friend Nag just wrote us a few lines from Calcutta, the first since he left Europe. He introduces a course at the University of Calcutta.

I believe Ollendorffs are considering translating your *Knulp* into French and publishing it – if you can come to an understanding with the publisher. But this volume would probably be a little short for a French edition. Do you have a story that could be published with it without destroying the general harmony? – Also, the publisher will write you.

And now we extend to you affectionate wishes for your news, "man of the forest"! So, you are marrying a dryad?

My sister and I thank you most sincerely.

Yours,

Romain Rolland

---

[1] The German edition of *Gandhi* was published by the Rotapfel Verlag, Zürich.

HERMANN HESSE TO ROMAIN ROLLAND

Delsberg (Delémont),
December 26, 1923.

Dear Romain Rolland,

For the three days of the Christmas holiday I am here in the Jura with my fiancée's parents. (On the table with my gifts lay the ten volumes of *Jean-Christophe*). And I send you from here my thanks for your charming, dear letter which gave me so much joy, as well as your work on Gandhi, which pleases me also because for once you parallel me in your Indian ways. Your interpretation of "Gandhiism" is European, and this must be so. The clarity of its formulations surpasses by far everything I have read elsewhere about it. And I like above all – apart from your clarity, intelligence and precision – the love and cordiality with which you, too, now embrace this distant world which has always been close to me.

You write that Ollendorff plans a French edition of my *Knulp*. Naturally this delights me. I haven't heard anything about it directly from Paris. But three weeks ago a lady, Geneviève Maury, also wrote me from Paris asking me for the translation rights for *Knulp*. I haven't answered her yet for I don't know if these two plans coincide only by chance or if they are identical. In case you should know something about it, please drop me a line.

Of course I could easily expand the French edition by adding another story.

As of tomorrow I'll be again in Basel, at the Krafft Hotel. In the near future I'll publish, at first only in a private edition of 250 copies, a new book entitled *Psychologia Balnearia, oder Glossen eines Kurgastes.**

For the New Year I wish you and your sister all the best and for myself the continuation of our friendship.

Sincerest greetings.

Yours,

Hermann Hesse

---

* *Psychologia Balnearia, or Notes by a Spa Visitor.*

ROMAIN ROLLAND'S DIARY

(December 1923) – . . . A renewed exchange of affectionate letters with Waldemar Bonsels and with Hermann Hesse. My sister and I are going to publish under the Ollendorff imprint some volumes of Hesse's tales and short stories. Hermann Hesse, who must be close to sixty, is going to marry again. – He sends me a beautiful aquarelle which he painted in the Tessin. – . . .

1924

HERMANN HESSE TO ROMAIN ROLLAND

Basel, Krafft Hotel,
3 March 1924.

Dear Friend,

Lying in bed with the 'flu for the second time this winter, I have been reading in the last few days the German translation of your *Annette and Sylvie*,* and I should like to tell you how much pleasure I had in accompanying you again on your purely poetic paths. This book is exceptionally dear to me, and I like in particular here again the purity and excellence of the plan and the precision of the expression. You know that I can also follow you into the intermediary region of the conflict between spirit and life, between thinking and art, and that I am familiar with the struggles and repressions of this intermediary realm. Therefore I was all the more delighted to discover that you devoted yourself so generously and sincerely to this graceful play. I do thank you for the joy this book brought me.

The translation is vivid and modern, but for my own taste it is too rough, too liberal in its choice of popular, vulgar expressions. Nevertheless it is quite good and intelligent. But something of the purity and conscious control of your language has been lost.

Something unexpected happened to me recently. Shortly after I had given Miss Maury permission to translate *Knulp,* I heard from a Mr. Knopff in Brussels whom I had also granted already this permission years ago. But I had forgotten him since he hadn't written me for several years. He writes me that he has now translated *Knulp,* but that he has no French publisher for the translation. I immediately wrote this to your friend, Miss Maury. I was hoping that an agreement or arrangement could still be worked out, but she hasn't answer me. I thought, for example, of the possibility of using Knopff's translation of *Knulp* and her translation of the other story?

This Belgian, whom I know only through some very sympathetic letters, asks me to inquire of you as to which of my books, besides *Knulp,* you consider most suitable for translation into French. I pass this question on and leave it up to you whether you'll reply to it or not. As far as I am concerned, I don't have any great ambitions, and I don't believe that my books could be effective in France at the present time.

And now I am once again sick in bed – as has happened already often this winter, and I long very much to be in Montagnola. I do hope you are well, and may you look often again at life with this passionate vision that is evident in your marvellous book.

Sincerely yours,

H. Hesse

---

* *The Enchanted Soul,* Vol. I.

ROMAIN ROLLAND TO HERMANN HESSE

Villeneuve, March 5, 1924.

Dear Friend,

I am glad you liked my *Annette et Sylvie,* and I hope that with its continuation (which has just appeared in French and which I will send you) you will become even more attached to my Annette: I have incarnated myself in her for such a long time – or rather, she incarnated herself in me – that I don't doubt that she really exists.

I'm afraid Miss Maury has already translated your *Knulp.*

You will have to come to an understanding with her. We unfortunate authors sometimes forget things. But it must be understood that, if within a given period (two years at most), the translator hasn't completed his task, he loses his rights. – Anyway, I can tell you that between Miss Maury and Knopff (both of whom I know) there is no doubt possible from a literary point of view. Miss Maury is an excellent writer (not only a translator, but also a recognized novelist). Her translations have an altogether different artistic value from Knopff's.

If you haven't heard from Miss Maury recently, it's because of a rather serious crisis in the Ollendorff Publishing House. It's going to be reorganized shortly, and they'll write to you. But I must tell you that Knopff wouldn't be accepted for the proposed series of translations.

After I have reflected on it, I'll write you as to which of your works I consider best suited for the French public.

Please help me. Tell me how *L'âme enchantée,* the general title of my series of novels – of which *Annette et Sylvie* is the first volume – is to be translated into German. (Without informing me of it, Kurt Wolff has omitted this title on his editions. I have just protested about it.) My translator, Paul Amann, doesn't know how to translate it. What word do you advise? "Verzauberte?" "Bezauberte?"... Your realize of course that it is a question of "enchantment" in the sense of "magic", of "illusion", of "Mayà". The soul forsakes its masks one by one. With every disguise that falls, it discovers yet another. Gradually, however, the soul progresses to deliverance. In short, the continuation of the work is the story of the long "disenchantment", of deliverance from the bonds of Mayâ.

Affectionate greetings and best wishes for your health. My health is all right, but precarious.

Yours,

Romain Rolland

HERMANN HESSE TO ROMAIN ROLLAND

Dear Friend,

Thank you for your dear, kind letter. Just after its arrival I woke up in a completely strange room with a poplar before the windows, for I had been taken to a clinic. I have been lying here already for a fortnight. But both my convalescence and springtime begin! I couldn't look forward to anything more beautiful than the continuation of your *Annette.*

Sincerest greetings.

Your friend

H. Hesse

Don't retract the title *Verzauberte Seele* (not *bezauberte*) for your magnificent book even if the translator has momentary doubts. This title – that expresses and yet conceals everything – is part of your beautiful music! May God bless you for it.

(Undated letter. Postmark: Basel, 10.III.1924.)

HERMANN HESSE TO ROMAIN ROLLAND

Dear R. Rolland,

For my sake, and for a dear Hindu who is here now, please write to let me know whether the news that the Mahatma is now in Switzerland is true. Where is he, or when does he arrive? My new Hindu friend asks many questions about you. And I am glad that I can hear once again the Indian intonation.

Most sincerely yours,

H. Hesse

(Undated Postcard. Postmark: Montagnola. 23.VII.24)

ROMAIN ROLLAND TO HERMANN HESSE

Villeneuve, 27.8.24

Dear Hermann Hesse,

There is no truth in this rumour! Gandhi is far too preoccupied by events in India to think of leaving his country now. The struggle between the two tendencies of the Swarajiste party is very serious; and Gandhi participates with all his energy. Every week he publishes his articles and speeches in his newspaper *Young India,* which is regularly sent to me from Madras. Gandhi has neither the time nor the inclination to spare himself and to take care of his health in Switzerland. I doubt even if he'll ever leave India again.

Affectionately yours,

Romain Rolland

1925

ROMAIN ROLLAND TO JEAN-RICHARD BLOCH

October 3, 1925

– If Miss Geneviève Maury brings the publisher a translation of *Knulp* by Hermann Hesse, I recommend the translator and the work to your readers. Hermann Hesse, whom Colin belittled because he doesn't write in line with the latest fashion, is an excellent writer of classical stature. His best stories may be put on the same shelf in the library as Gottfried Keller's and Goethe's.

ROMAIN ROLLAND TO GENEVIEVE MAURY

Villeneuve, Villa Olga,
November 10, 25.

– I have written to Jean-Richard Bloch, urging him particularly with regard to *Knulp*. On October 23 he replied:

– *I forwarded to Bazalgette what you said about* Knulp. *You'll recall that you spoke to me about it already two years ago in Villeneuve. Upon my return I immediately spoke about it to the persons concerned. The appropriate channels have therefore been opened.*

You should therefore write to Bazalgette (59, rue Rennequin, XVIIIe). Indicate in your letter to him that you know that he has already been notified by Jean-Richard Bloch and by myself.

1926

HERMANN HESSE TO ROMAIN ROLLAND

Temporary address:
Zurich, Schanzengraben 31.

Dear Romain Rolland,

I address myself to you to request a small favour. I don't have the address of our friend Kalidas Nag. Kindly forward him the enclosed printed matter which may please him.

Oh yes, now it is also timely to congratulate you on your sixtieth birthday. I wouldn't like to give voice to pompous expressions about this. Instead I'd like to say that on this occasion, as indeed always, I think of you with the sincerest friendship.

Since my life has once again become very difficult for me, I have been travelling for the past few months and was again in Baden and also in Southern Germany. I expect to stay away for a while longer yet, but intend to return again to Montagnola in the Spring.

Farewell for now. I hope you are well or that your life is at least bearable, and may you experience joy on your birthday!

Most sincerely yours,

Hermann Hesse

(Undated letter. Postmark: Zurich, 22.I.26)

ROMAIN ROLLAND TO HERMANN HESSE

Villeneuve, January 23, 1926.

Dear Hermann Hesse,

Here is Kalidas Nag's address:

91 Upper Circular Road
Calcutta.

I'm forwarding your article to him.

You know, don't you, about his marriage to Santa Chatterjee, the daughter of the director of the *Modern Review?*

I think the French translation of *Siddhartha* has been forwarded to you. The prudent Grasset[1] omitted the dedication for fear of compromising himself! You see, in Paris they are still at it. My name is avoided like the pest.

What I read between your lines saddens me. May the eyes' delight, which is always expressed at the beginning of your letter[2], restore your happiness and peace of mind!

Thank you for your good wishes.

Affectionately yours,

Romain Rolland

---

[1] The French Publisher.
[2] Hesse frequently embellished his letters with a small aquarelle.

HERMANN HESSE TO ROMAIN ROLLAND

Zurich, Schanzengraben 31.

Dear Romain Rolland, dear Friend and Colleague,

It was very kind of you to forward not only to Nag the printed matter, but to send me also greetings.

I didn't know anything about the publication of the French *Siddhartha.* I was able to find a copy here in a bookstore and bought it. It's true, the dedication has been omitted! I, too, sincerely regret this. Fortunately the translator indicated at least in his preface that I had dedicated the book to you.

I can imagine very vividly your position vis-à-vis the French majority. During the war my own relationship with official Germany was quite similar. But then I was lucky that my fatherland lost the war. Thus the same persons, who in the reverse situation would have put me against the wall and executed me, now read my books and praise me.

It's bitter that this should be so, but these situations don't deserve to be taken seriously. They are characteristic neither of France nor of our time, but they have been with us since time immemorial and are characteristic only of the human species.

I am enclosing for you also a short essay which will give you some insight into my present life. I am going through some difficult times and every day I take up life only with reluctance. But from time to time I laugh again and have moments of wisdom and humour.

The preface by the translator of *Siddhartha* is well-meant. But as far as its dates and facts are concerned, it isn't at all reliable. Quite a lot of it is imagined – anyway I wanted to tell you this.

Most sincerely yours,

Hermann Hesse

1928

ROMAIN ROLLAND TO PAUL AMANN

January 26, 1928.

. . . – No, I haven't seen Hermann Hesse for a long time. He always withdraws. I wait for his unstable mood to bring him back to his starting-point. His art becomes always more perfect. In *Steppenwolf* there are some moving confessions. But basically he is so weak, this false wolf! this lamb from the Parnassus of the Golden Hill (Lugano). He follows every trend – be it literary, moral, or beyond morality – however depraved or mundane it may be. – And he is so naïve! I am very much afraid that as the good German he is, he does in earnest what our young people merely voice. That's enough intoxication and more! If he were now to use cocaine!... The whole ending of *Steppenwolf* distresses me (also from a literary, or rather intellectual, point of view) and makes me shrug my shoulders. That's fine when one is 20 years old! But at the age of 50! – It's no good, no matter what they say, to be (or to want to be) a perpetual adolescent – with all the problems of a brain between seventeen and twenty-five years old. We must have the courage to act our age. Nothing is lost by it. But our man in his fifties is obsessed by middle age love and even old age love... – I have read some of Hesse's recent poetry which is admirable and poignant. – Fortunately by nature an artist is like a cat which, when it's thrown out of the house, always lands on its feet. But he must be careful! A tragic old age is in store for him.

1931

ROMAIN ROLLAND TO MADELEINE ROLLAND

Lugano, Tuesday, August 18, 1931.

– . . . I was pleased to see Montagnola again. We stayed for an hour on the terrace of the little hotel that's situated above a mass of verdure, vineyards, chestnuts, pink or red houses and above the arm of the lake which turns in on itself and looks like a big, lost pond. The air was much lighter than in Lugano. High up in the country Hermann Hesse had a little new country house built for himself. I've been told that he has just returned to the country. I'll probably drop him a line. – . . .

ROMAIN ROLLAND TO HERMANN HESSE

Lugano, Park Hotel,
Thursday, August 20, 1931.

Dear Hermann Hesse,

I spent the other day in Montagnola and a villa at the top of the Golden Hill was pointed out to me as being your home. But I didn't want to disturb you there.

If you happen to come down to Lugano in the near future, I would be very pleased if you would have lunch with me (12.30 p.m.) at the Park Hotel. I would be very happy to see you again.

If that's not possible, I'm sending you at least greetings with my affection that the years of silence hasn't diminished.

Faithfully yours,

Romain Rolland

HERMANN HESSE TO ROMAIN ROLLAND

Dearest Romain Rolland,

What a joy! Thank you very much for your kind letter! You are always heartily welcome. Do arrange it so that your road takes you once again to Montagnola. We have only just now moved into our new home (it belongs to a friend in Zurich who furnished it for me). Unfortunately I hurt myself as we moved in, so that I can't come to Lugano now. I can walk only with difficulty. But here you'll always find me and my friend Ninon, and my heart and home are always open to you. You could telephone also my friend (Lugano No. ....) But please don't reveal this unlisted number to anyone.

I do hope to see you. Please decide yourself as to the day and time.

Greeting you with affection and respect,

Yours,

H. Hesse

(Undated letter. Postmark: Montagnola, 21.VIII.1931)

ROMAIN ROLLAND TO MADELEINE ROLLAND

Park Hotel, Lugano
Saturday, August 22, 31.

– ... Hermann Hesse, to whom I had written, replied by return mail in a very affectionate letter telling me how pleased he would be to receive me in his new home. He just moved there and hurt his foot so that he can't come to Lugano. He indicates his friend's nickname who is the lady of the house. She is called "Ninon". All he needs to do now is to call the house "The Enclosure"* – I'll call on him next week. – Today we intend to visit once again the church in Morcote. – ...

* A pun on Ninon de Lenclos (l'enclos, i.e., the enclosure).

ROMAIN ROLLAND TO HERMANN HESSE

Lugano, Park Hotel,
August 22, 1931.

Dear Friend,

Thank you for your kind letter. I expect to stay here for another week. Early next week I'll come with the three o'clock bus to see you. I'll let you know in the morning by phone, calling at the Lugano number you indicated to me (I won't tell anyone about it). I'll take the liberty of coming with a Russian friend, who helps me with my work, and who admires and loves your books. Her name is Maria Koudacheff.

And so, farewell for the present.

Affectionately yours,

Romain Rolland

ROMAIN ROLLAND TO MADELEINE ROLLAND

Lugano, Park Hotel,
August 23, 1931.

– ... Hesse contacted me by phone yesterday through his Ninon. He seems very eager to see me. He was afraid I would leave suddenly. I'll go tomorrow if it isn't raining or cool.

ROMAIN ROLLAND TO JEAN GUEHENNO

Lugano, Park Hotel,
August 26, 1931.

... You should contact Stefan Zweig who has been ignored too much by *Europe* and who is offended as a result. He would certainly bring out the European and contemporary meaning of Goethe in German-speaking regions. Perhaps Hermann Hesse. I'm going to see him today ...

ROMAN ROLLAND'S DIARY

(August 26, 1931.) – Hermann Hesse has returned to Montagnola. Letters and telephones. He manifests a great desire to see me again. I'm going to visit him with Macha. Hesse is with a friend. I only know her nickname: Ninon. She waits for us at the bus stop to direct us to the house. She is a woman of about thirty-five, not pretty, with a broad face, rather common features, with a dark complexion – the Tessinian type (although she is certainly not Tessinian, but probably from southern Germany). But she appears kind and intelligent and her brown eyes are lit up by her smile. In the course of our conversation, I learn that she was in Montagnola, and in the same house as Hesse (that means before his second marriage). A rich friend generously gave Hesse a plot of land he owned in Montagnola as a present and provided the necessary funds for the construction of a house which was built according to Hesse's plans. And he promised Hesse its use as long as he lives. The site is the most beautiful one you could see on this charming Golden Hill. It's outside Montagnola high up (at the turn of the road that leads to Agra). It's sheltered both from the wind and the noise of traffic by a belt of chestnuts. At the same time there is a clear view from all the other sides, and the apricot-coloured house, which is quite isolated because of the esplanade, dominates the entire region. On three sides the beautiful lake extends right up to the foot of the "Piccolo Mondo Antico" and the mountains, some of which are shaped like the Appenines of Tuscany. And all around, along the slopes, is the rich country of the Tessin that abound with fruit trees: the high vineyards and fig trees, the trees from the land of Canaan. Hesse and his companion enjoy like children this beautiful new home, which they themselves have planned. (The move is not yet completed. They have worn themselves out in the house and garden: Hesse is dragging his leg). It's delightful to behold their naïve joy. The first thing Hesse points out to me is the independence of the two companions which is guaranteed (is it actually real?) by the (relative) independence of the two apartments. Each has a separate entrance (but they are connected in the middle by some rooms). Hesse's quarters look out on Lugano and Montagnola, Ninon's on the S. Salvatore and the Mte. Generoso. (Ninon – even more than Hesse – seems to be in love with silence – she has a strange need for complete visual and auditory solitude, the forests, the bare mountainsides, the wide spaces unspoiled by man).

Hesse, who came to meet us on the path of his property, is bare-headed. He wears his grey hair in a crew cut. His face is thin and lined. His mouth is thin-lipped, wide and tense, but smiling with us. He wears glasses. His white suit and gardening shoes are worn, spotted and not well brushed. He has kind, affectionate, and smiling eyes. As far as his mental state is concerned, I find him much happier and much more balanced than ever before. He speaks (expressing himself with difficulty in French) confidently and freely. He no longer reveals any traces of his past crises. (Apparently) he doesn't deny anything of his earlier philosophy, but he harmonizes it with his new life that is without any dogma. He is still very much taken up with sketching and painting. He says the source of this vocation goes back to the most gloomy period of the war when he was close to death. The purity of colour was a refuge for him. No more thinking! And he continues to engross himself in it when he is intellectually exhausted. (One sees on his face traces of the mental sterility against which he fights successfully). He doesn't speak about his poetical works. But it is clear that in this area he is diametrically opposed to my art. He has to defend himself too much against the burden of social realities to grant it recognition in his poetry. And, incidentally, speaking of the young who address themselves to him asking whether they can become poets, Hesse replies: – "Yes, provided you commit yourself not to preoccupy yourself with the troubles of the world situation." – But that's just an inadvertent remark. And throughout the remainder of our discussion, he seems to think along the same lines as I do (but I don't ask him about it). – In the evening, Hesse says they read together. His companion reads to him in German Tolstoy's *War and Peace.* He re-reads it every seven years and is always equally moved by it. He says that whereas when one reads Dostoevsky and closes the book, one can hardly remember a character – one doesn't distinguish one person from the others and all together they aren't distinct from the general atmosphere that represents the soul of the poet. In Tolstoy's works, every one of his characters, even the least significant and most transient, is described separately and is immortal. "More sculptured than painted", adds Hesse's intelligent companion. – Tea and cake is served. (No wine, out of consideration for me. – I tell them they are mistaken. I remind them that, thank God, I am a Burgundian!) And as Hesse awkwardly passes the cups around, he excuses himself by saying with charming naïvete: "I am still a novice in my role as *capitalist...*" – A very ample library, still only half-organized, that includes many works from the Orient. – Beautiful rooms, well-lighted, looking out on the vast panorama and the bright sky of Swiss Italy. No musical instrument. No radio. Noise is not allowed to penetrate here. – Few literary friendships, I think. Hesse had been elected to the German Academy in Berlin but he resigned from it.

ROMAIN ROLLAND TO MADELEINE ROLLAND

Park Hotel, Lugano,
Thursday, August 27, 31.

– . . . Yesterday in splendid weather we went on another excursion to Montagnola. The atmosphere was especially light because a warm wind blew over the hills. Ninon waited for us at the station and led us to the house. It's impossible to imagine a more beautiful location. It's outside the little town, right on top of the Golden Hill, but protected by a thick curtain of chestnut-trees. The apricot-coloured house (with a two-faced Janus-like front) faces with the one side towards Lugano which dominates the entire region and the late right up to the foot of the "Piccolo Mondo Antico", and the other side faces towards the Mte. S. Salvatore which dominates the slopes of vineyards, fig trees, and meadows. Hesse is very lucky. A rich friend put the lot and the necessary funds at his disposal to build the house according to his own plans and to furnish it. The house is for Hesse's use as long as he lives. The house has been built for both of them with love under Hesse's and Ninon's directions. Each of them has a separate entrance and wing of the house, while they have at the same time a common apartment. Who is this Ninon? I have not been able to discover her real name. But I was surprised to learn that ten years ago she was in the same house as Hesse (in another house in the village) in Montagnola – that means even before Hesse's second marriage. Ninon is about thirty-five years old, not beautiful in the ordinary sense. She is dark, has a broad face, and rather strong features. But her expression is intelligent and good-natured, and her eyes are illuminated by her smiles. It's a delight to see how she enjoys their new home in which they both worked untiringly – not only in the house, but also in the garden. Ninon seems to have a passion for solitude and silence that's even greater than Hesse's – it's almost morbid. The façade of the house she chose for herself doesn't overlook anything of Lugano or Montagnola, but looks out on woods and the broad horizon.

Hesse is thin and pale; but he has a better mental outlook (if I may say so). He is more "chatty", and seems happier than on all previous occasions I've seen him. He, too, experiences a naïve joy in his little new palace. When he offered us tea, he excused himself with a smile for being still a novice in his new role of "capitalist".

We stayed about two or three hours, associated in a very affectionate friendship, and were cheerful and talkative. – We agreed that they would both come and spend an afternoon with us before we leave.

Hesse still corresponds with Nag. But he mainly sees some Japanese. It seemed to me that he doesn't deny any of his past ideas, but that he has succeeded in harmonizing them with his present life. He now enjoys a well-balanced state of mind. He has a son who studies architecture in Paris, for whom Le Corbusier is a god. – ...

HERMANN HESSE TO ROMAIN ROLLAND

(Late August, 1931.)

Dear Mr. Rolland,

I had intended to visit you tomorrow or the day after tomorrow. But now visitors have announced their stay here for several days and great demands are made upon me.

I am very grateful that we have met again. It gives me great pleasure and confirms some of the best in me.

Sincerest greetings and best wishes,

Yours,

Hermann Hesse

ROMAIN ROLLAND TO HERMANN HESSE

Lugano Park Hotel,
Wednesday, September 2, 31.

Dear Friend,

I had asked my sister to send you from Villeneuve a copy of my new *Goethe and Beethoven.* She couldn't find one and therefore sent me instead this volume which has just been published by René Arcos, under the Sablier imprint. Please accept it in the meantime. Once I've returned to Villeneuve, I'll get the *G. & B.* – And don't hold my portraits, reproduced in this book, against me. I wasn't consulted about the illustrations. Oh, I would so much more prefer to see my text encircled with a vine-trellis from the Golden Hill, or with plum or apricot-coloured houses – a feast for the eyes. But I don't have your talent for drawing, nor your fingers. Mine are only good on the piano.

I am very happy about the afternoon we spent together. I sincerely thank you and your kind companion.

Faithfully yours,

Romain Rolland

(My permanent address is still Villeneuve (Vaud), Villa Olga.)

Please think about the idea I suggested to you as I was about to leave – a personal tribute to Goethe. And if the editor of the *Europe* review, my friend the writer Jean Guéhenno (one of the few authors of the young literary generation in Paris whom I admire), writes you about this, do look on his request favourably.

I just received a telegram from Gandhi which was sent from his boat. He'll be arriving in Marseilles on the 11th. I'll probably meet him along the way between Dijon and Calais.

HERMANN HESSE TO ROMAIN ROLLAND

Dear Romain Rolland,

Sincerest thanks for your last letter from Lugano and for your beautiful, precious gift. I am reading it with great interest.

When you were here, I had wanted to speak to you about the forthcoming low-priced edition of my *Siddhartha.* I had intended to tell you that I remembered you once again in my Foreword – you to whom Part I had been dedicated earlier.

In the meantime I received a copy of the Foreword of this book, and I'm enclosing it herewith for you. It's not that I attach great value to this text – but I want to show you that the delightful renewal of our friendship thanks to our last meeting wasn't necessary to remind me of you often and always with the same affection and admiring fellowship.

Most sincerely yours,

Hermann Hesse

(Undated letter. Postmark: Montagnola. September 7, 1931)

HERMANN HESSE TO ROMAIN ROLLAND

Montagnola, October 7, 1931.

Dear Mr. Rolland,

I have hesitated a long time about writing the promised essay on my relationship to Goethe.[1] I am enclosing it herewith and ask you to please forward it to Paris.

As far as the honorarium is concerned, I agree, of course, in advance to your review's customary arrangements. I would also appreciate receiving some off-prints after its publication.

The sun is shining continually and the *Föhn* blows frequently, but it is always dry and often warm. For three days we picked grapes. My son helped, too. Now I'll stay here till the end of the month, then I'll go away for the winter. My address for the winter months is Zurich, Schanzengraben 31.

Sincerest greetings.

Faithfully yours,

H. Hesse

---

[1] "Dank an Goethe", written as a tribute for the centennial of Goethe's death for *Europe*, Paris.

ROMAIN ROLLAND TO HERMANN HESSE

Villeneuve, Villa Olga
October 8, 1931.

Dear Friend,

Thank you for your *Dankgesang** to the Divinity whose brilliance is the source of Goethe's genius. Yes, I share your sentiment. We can love perfectly only those in whom we perceive Tao's mysterious glance.

– I forward your manuscript to Jean Guéhenno, the editor of *Europe*. He'll certainly write you to come to an understanding with you.

Our Lake Geneva is very beautiful. It plays Veronese melodies for us. – But I caught another dose of bronchitis in the damp air. I miss Lugano's sunshine.

Affectionately yours,

Romain Rolland

---

* Eulogy

ROMAIN ROLLAND TO JEAN GUEHENNO

Villeneuve (Vaud),
Villa Olga,
October 8, 1931.

Dear Friend,

I have already received for your Goethe issue an excellent essay by Hermann Hesse: *"Dank an Goethe"*. I am enjoying it before forwarding it to you. A very good translator will have to be found for it. – ...

1932

HERMANN HESSE TO ROMAIN ROLLAND

Zurich, January 15, 1932.

Dear Mr. Rolland,

The Rotapfel Verlag sent me some proofs of your German edition of your war articles. At the same time they write to me that this edition causes them great concern and that they consider it necessary to tone down the text and to make certain cuts, because in its present form the book would be rejected in Germany today.

I, too, believe that this would be so. But I would have taken this risk nevertheless. I am enclosing herewith my reply to your publisher. He had requested me to act as mediator with you. It seems to me that the two words I have referred to really can be dispensed with. The expression *"Hunnen"** is not worthy of you, my respected friend, and it would apply equally well to isolated examples of excesses perpetrated by your compatriots during the occupation of the Ruhr. Men are like beasts when they have no star to look up to. But we must nor reproach one nation with the monopoly of bestiality. And as far as the second word is concerned,** I would advise you to omit it too; these events are altogether too obscure.

As far as the rest is concerned, I am, as always, in complete agreement with you, as you see from my letter to the publisher, of which I enclose a copy.

My letter is written somewhat haphazardly and in a hurry. I am in the process of packing. Next week I'll be in St. Moritz (Engadine), Chantarella Hotel. My wife will accompany me and sends you kind regards.

We saw my ophthalmologist, a genius, in Germany. He thinks my eyesight is seriously endangered. But he hopes to save it through his treatments. However this will require years of patience.

Best wishes.

Sincerely yours,

H. Hesse

---

* Huns

** *prémédité*

HERMANN HESSE TO THE ROTAPFEL VERLAG, ZURICH.

Zurich, January 15, 1932.

Confidential.

Gentlemen,

I have read your letter and also the controversial passages in Rolland's book. From a commercial point of view I fully understand your hesitations. But I share with Rolland his way of seeing things. My point of view regarding this is as follows:

1. Before you agree to have Rolland's book published, your reader absolutely must reread once again Rolland's articles on the war.

2. These articles are not by any means simple, autobiographical testimonials which must be protected against any falsification. They are much more than that. They are the testimony of the most serious and most noble attempt to arouse people's consciences at the beginning of the World War.

It's a moral obligation that these two things will not be forgotten by the world: that Rolland wrote these articles and that Gerhard Hauptmann lamentably avoided responding to the noble call.[1] Everything that is young and good in this world is here on Rolland's side.

3. The military activities which Rolland designates in his articles as "crimes" are indeed so in reality.

If in the Treaty of Versailles, France didn't show itself a few years later in a generous and noble light, but was mean and cruel, these German "crimes" have thereby been compensated for and punished to some degree. But because of this, the Treaty of Versailles certainly does not in any way deserve to be called a "crime". It is a treaty, and it was accepted and signed by Germany.

4. Although I don't find all of Rolland's expressions pleasant and although I detect a certain element of rhetoric, there are really only two expressions which I find truly reproachable.

On page 68 the expression "The Huns". It's unworthy of Rolland. And on page 70 in the last line the word premeditated". I, too, would have willingly omitted these two words in the book; as far as the others are concerned – no.

You see, I agree with Rolland who doesn't consent to toning down the text, although this must now seem timely. Rolland is right.

Another question: generally speaking, should this volume be published now? At the present time there is in Germany not the least feeling that, just like the other countries, Germany also is largely responsible for the war. Nor is there an awareness that because of this, from a moral standpoint it has deserved to a large extent the Treaty of Versailles. Germany rejected the appeal to its conscience made by Rolland in 1914/15. It spurned it and agreed with G. Hauptmann who was of the opinion that these matters didn't concern him.

A positive response to this book cannot be expected from Germany at the present time.

I agree therefore all the more with Rolland if he insists

that his text must stand as it is, even if it means that the German edition can be published only later.[2]

Yours truly,

Hesse

Please consider this letter confidential. I authorize you to forward it only to Rolland.

---

[1] "Lettre à Gerhart Hauptmann", in *Au-dessus de la mêlée*
[2] *Au-dessus de la mêlée* was published in Germany only in 1967.

ROMAIN ROLLAND TO HERMANN HESSE

Villeneuve (Vaud), Villa Olga,
January 20, 1932.

Dear Friend,

Thank you kindly for having sent me your reply to Dr. Eugen Rentsch, the Director of the Rotapfel Verlag. I didn't know that he approached German writers to try to be awarded a *satisfecit** of a good German citizen.

I am glad you agree with me. But let me explain to you the exact conditions for this publication. I wager Dr. Rentsch took great care not to reveal them.

The German book must include the two series of French articles I had published during the war under the title: *Au-dessus de la mêlée* – and *Les Précurseurs.* (They succeed each other – the first was written in 1914 and 1915 – and the second was written between 1916 and 1918). I added to these articles for the German edition a long introductory essay, entitled "Adieu au Passé"**. (It was published in French under this title in *Europe* in its edition of June 15, 1931.) In this introductory article I recall my state of mind which gave rise to these first articles. I confess there without mercy my guilt and indict that period. I don't hide any of my mistakes. I show how much difficulty I had freeing myself from the thick clouds of ignorance massed together for us by the governments and by their press – but how I looked unceasingly and in spite of all obstacles and threats for the dangerous truth. I show how my thinking has changed from the first articles in August and September 1914, which were written without a guide and in ignorance – as I was absolutely alone in my thinking – up to the end of the war. My thinking hasn't ceased evolving in a direction that is more detached from any fatherland and one that is more revolutionary. And this evolution has progressed without interruption since the end of the war until now. (I indicate this in the last pages of my Introduction – by declaring that I would subsequently write a second article on the period from 1919 to 1932 which hasn't been for me the period of the least struggles.)

Therefore there can be no doubt as to how I personally judge my first articles on the war. I myself denounce today their exaggerations and errors. – *But I do not have the right to change them.* They are historical texts. I have written them. *I must accept responsibility for them.* I am not one of those who flee from the responsibility for what they have done. *I have done it. Let me be judged on what I have done!* Even if I regret it today, I am not allowed to say: "I didn't do it!" – I hate lies and cowardice. I will not change a single word of what I have written.

– . . . As far as the word *Huns* is concerned which can't displease you more than myself – let's re-establish the circumstances leading to the writing of the article: 1) Hauptmann had just had this tragi-comic dispute with Bergson in which the word "barbarians" had been exchanged. – 2) As the note on page one of my "*Lettre ouverte à Hauptmann*"*** indicates (I don't know what the German translation did with it, for the translation was not submitted to me) the Wolff agency in Berlin (those idiots) had perversely sought to frighten Europe by announcing that *the old city of Louvain, so rich in art works, didn't exist any more today!!* (sic) And I had just read this bulletin in the *Gazette de Lausanne* of August 29, 1914. That Germany seemed to praise itself for having destroyed a whole city "rich in art works" left me speechless. How could one not think of Attila? (Not for a moment would it have entered my mind – nor that of any Swiss or Frenchman – that an official German Agency could, out of stupidity, have invented such an outrageous crime!) And I wrote to Hauptmann: *I know the intellectual and moral grandeur of your powerful race ... But by what name do you want to be called today? ... Are you the heirs of Goethe, or those of Attila? ...* – And further on: – *I am not addressing myself against you to the opinion of the rest of the world. I am appealing to you personally, Hauptmann ... Voice your protest against such a crime! If you do not do so, you show either that you approve of it or that you are too weak to raise your voice against the Huns who are in authority over you ...*

(I am quoting the French text literally. The term *Huns* doesn't refer to the German people, but *to the military leaders* who could give the orders for this devastation. – Moreover, don't think that I would hesitate to apply it to the Frenchmen who bombarded from their planes the little children in Karlsruhe! I know today where I stand with regard to European inhumanity, without national distinctions.)

But what do you think Hauptmann answered me? – This – I read it in an Italian newspaper of September 12, 1914 (*Corriere della Sera*) which was at that time friendly toward the Germans:

... *Call, if you like,* sons of Attila *the soldiers of our glorious Landwehr! We are content if they break the vicious circle of our enemies. And it's much better that you should call us* sons of Attila *by remaining inside your borders than if you came to write a sentimental epitaph on our grave by calling us* sons of Goethe.

I don't say that Hauptmann is altogether wrong! But you, my dear friend, realize that he seemed to accept more calmly this attribute (with which I didn't designate him! but which I beseeched him to prove false) than Dr. Eugen Rentsch, the faithful defender of German honour – some fifteen years later.

Affectionate greetings. The news you write about your health distresses me very much. Your eyesight is precious for us. Do spare your eyes!

Your devoted friend,

Romain Rolland

Please extend kind regards to your companion.

---

* Good record.
** "Good-bye to the Past"
*** "Open Letter to Hauptmann"

HERMANN HESSE TO ROMAIN ROLLAND

Chantarella,
January 22, 1932.

Dear Friend and honoured Comrade,

I studied your letter carefully and I agree with you wholeheartedly.

If I have so little liking for the word "Huns", it isn't only because of its application in certain circles today, but I feel sorry for the sake of the Huns themselves whose blind advance in spite of everything is magnificent and which has the character of a natural phenomenon rather than that of an amoral quality.

But I grant you that the text of your essays doesn't allow even for the slightest further attenuation.

I don't know if you realize how much I experienced and shared with you your fate on a small scale. I have never been as exposed as you, although I've made a lot of enemies for myself. But I have experienced the war here almost exactly as you did, and even now my relations with my compatriots are just as they were in 1914. The war meant for my private life a rude awakening to reality in its essence and to the tragedy of life and of the spirit. Your letter to Hauptmann is therefore for me a document that is unique and of the greatest importance. And both your appeal and Hauptmann's failure to respond are unforgettable for me and have become symbolic for many things.

If I got involved in the Rotapfel affair at all, it certainly wasn't for the sake of this editor, but because I had grave misgivings that in the end your essays wouldn't be published at all in the light of today's mentality in Germany, and that would be a great pity.

My wife thanks you for your greetings. In November we got married in Montagnola.

We expect to stay up here until the end of February. Then we'll be a few weeks in Zurich, and from mid-April on we'll stay again permanently in Montagnola. I would be truly delighted to see you again there or anywhere else.

Should this publication of your essays in German be in jeopardy and should I be able to do something to help you, I am always at your service. The publisher's hesitations are certainly only purely commercial ones. He is afraid that he will be blacklisted and boycotted in Germany on which he is dependent for his sales. Unfortunately he has grounds for his fears. Morally speaking Germany is even sicker now than in 1914. It has forgotten everything it could have learnt through the war and its consequences.

Faithfully yours,

H. Hesse

HERMANN HESSE: CULTURAL AND ART BOOKS*

The Frenchman Romain Rolland who was once celebrated throughout the world as the author of the great musical novel *Jean-Christophe* and as the winner of the Nobel Prize (which he donated immediately to the Red Cross, for this was in 1914) is among those authors of our time whose influence has extended far beyond literature. And Romain Rolland is today almost better known as a friend of Gandhi, as the champion of the oppressed, as the protector of young talents, and above all as the enemy and implacable critic of the spirit that gives rise to wars. May the literary work of this noble personality be once again remembered above everything else.

What leads me to say this is the popular, low-priced German edition of *Jean-Christophe* in three large volumes which Rütten and Loening in Frankfurt has published and which deserves only praise. In his essence Rolland has developed through his music. He was once Professor of the history of music at the Sorbonne. Among Romain Rolland's fictional works, *Jean-Christophe, The Market Place* and *The Enchanted Soul* are the major and most important ones. *Jean-Christophe,* which comprises several volumes, is the story of a musician, a work of majestic humaneness that abounds in courageous accusations against today's thinking. The series of novels of *The Enchanted Soul* is still incomplete. But the author expects to finish its last volumes this year. The first three volumes have been published in German by Engelhorn in Stuttgart. They are entitled, *Annette and Sylvie, Summer,* and *Mother and Son.* Each of these novels may be read independently and may, of course, also be purchased separately. They were well presented by Engelhorn. – ... Let me remind you also of the charming but tragic idyll *Pierre and Luce* (also published in German by Engelhorn). It's a beautifully moving wartime story which is illustrated with woodcuts by Masereel. In *The Enchanted Soul* Rolland, who is a great admirer of the master Tolstoy, created once again – as he had in the story of the hero's in *Jean-Christophe* – a great number of scenes and characters whose grace and ingenuity bring to mind the unforgettable female characters in *War and Peace.* – In Paris it's fashionable today among the young writers to speak of Rolland as someone of respectable, but outmoded greatness. This indicates that since the war French literature on the whole is hardly interested in humanism. In Russia, in India, and in Japan the young know Romain Rolland's name, and he represents for them much more than a name. Among the great Frenchmen of the same generation,

André Gide alone may be compared with him, apart from the late Proust.

---

* Published in *Propyläen,* Munich, October 10, 1932.

HERMANN HESSE: ROMAIN ROLLAND AND MALWIDA VON MEYSENBUG*

Twice in his youth Rolland had the opportunity of receiving the kind of initiation that strengthened him in his mission and to some extent made him a devotee in the anonymous world alliance of idealists: thanks to the famous letter of the aged Tolstoy and thanks to his friendship with Malwida, the old lady who had been the fraternal, and soon maternal, friend of Wagner and of Nietzsche. Rolland's correspondence with Malwida von Meysenbug – who is the author of the *Memoirs of an Idealist* which have not yet been forgotten – represents therefore, apart from its biographical significance, a work of merit and a symbol. The present volume, which contains about half of this beautiful, moving correspondence, reveals to us the development of a friendship between an ardent young man and a noble, cultured old lady who introduces him with an almost patriachal gesture into the community of great minds and shares with him her spiritual heritage. There is already something historical in this belated echo of the days of Romanticism and emotion. This volume provides a wealth of illustrations of Rolland's bonds with that tradition and his relationships with Beethoven, Tolstoy, and Wagner that are almost like those of a personal disciple. Malwida's letter of May 28, 1890, which is the first truly affectionate letter, reveals something of the devotion of another period and another culture, and reminds one somehow of the correspondence between Goethe and Schiller. These reminiscences of a biographical, historical, and cultural nature are obviously something respectable and beautiful. But in today's unsettled world they would be of little interest if Rolland were merely a writer interested in the present, if he were merely a famous man – For a large part of the literary youth in France, Rolland represents a kind of past grandeur. The Rolland who in Asia, in Russia, and in other countries far away from France is today one of the most read and most influential writers, having separated himself long ago from France as well as from the literary caste, is for many Frenchmen nothing more than a more or less definite memory of the author of *Jean-Christophe* and of a Nobel Prize winner. The merit and the influence that Rolland's personality has had for a very long time and throughout a large part of the world can never be fully expressed in his literary work. Since Rolland in 1914 became the advocate and protector of oppressed humanity and endangered humanism – quite above any literature, he is also above politics, an idea or rather a symbol, a monument that bears the name of Romain Rolland and which has been representing for at least two generations a banner and a torch. From this point of view the historical figure of the Rolland of this correspondence also becomes meaningful, profoundly meaningful, and a unique phenomenon.

---

* Published in the *Neue Zürcher Zeitung*, November 22, 1932.

1933

HERMANN HESSE TO ROMAIN ROLLAND

Spring 1933

Dear Mr. Romain Rolland,

During the last three months, I have often thought of you in friendship. Once again I had to relive the experiences of 1914. I had to free myself of the sentimentalities and sophisms of patriotism and nevertheless felt like an accomplice of the new attack against humanity and the Spirit.

Today I am approaching you merely with a friendly and harmless mission. In the name of the printer Graf, I have to forward you the enclosed pamphlet.[1] It has been published in a very limited quantity by the students of a trade school in Gotha, and their director asked me to dedicate also a copy to you for he has great admiration for you. His address is Reinhardsbrunner Str. 31, Gotha.

This pamphlet is not for sale. It's an experimental work accomplished by apprentices, and a document reflecting the state of mind of a very small circle of workers who love you.

Since March we have been continually disturbed in Montagnola. The German refugees arrive in great numbers; some of them have stayed as our guests for a long time.

Cordial and respectful greetings,

Yours,

H. Hesse

---

[1] *Mahnung* (Warning)

ROMAIN ROLLAND TO HERMANN HESSE

Park Hotel, Lugano
Wednesday, September 13, 1933

Dear Friend,

I have been in Lugano for two weeks and will be here for another week (until the 21 or 22). There hasn't been a single day when I didn't think of visiting you with my companion Marie Koudachef. But my very poor health has so far prevented me from doing so. And on top of everything else the poor weather of the past few days brought on a slight attack of gastric 'flu from which I have not yet fully recovered.

If my health and time will allow it, I will try to visit you before my departure. Let me know if any specific days are more convenient for you – or if in general you don't have some commitment.

In case it would definitely be impossible for me to meet you, I would regret it profoundly and assure you of my loyal friendship. Please extend kind regards to Mrs. Hermann Hesse from myself and cordial greetings from Mrs. Marie Koudachef.

Faithfully yours,

Romain Rolland

Thank you for your letter this Spring with the book of poems it recommended to me. Having been sick then, burdened with work, and about to leave Villeneuve, I still haven't been able to read the book: I apologize to you. – I had the pleasure of seeing Moïssi a few days ago.

ROMAIN ROLLAND TO MADELEINE ROLLAND

Park Hotel, Lugano
Saturday, September 16, 1933.

– . . . Your letter is late today. I am waiting for it. – Besides, I wouldn't trust the Lugano mail too much. I have several examples of letters (especially from Lugano for Lugano itself) which were delayed or lost. (Negligence or censorship?) – It's very odd that Hermann Hesse didn't answer the letter I wrote him three days ago. But yesterday I received a strange letter from a young lady whom I don't know (but whose father was perhaps the manager of the Mooser Hotel in Vevey in 1914 and manages or managed, since then, a hotel here, in Paradiso): she says that "her (our) car" (the hotel's car?) will take me to Hermann Hesse. Does she therefore know about my letter to Hesse? Then why didn't he write me? – Anyway, I won't take any cars in Lugano I don't know. The mail bus is good enough for me. – ...

ROMAIN ROLLAND TO MADELEINE ROLLAND

Park Hotel, Lugano,
Sunday, September 17, 1933.

– . . . Yesterday evening Mrs. Hermann Hesse telephoned me and we agreed that we would visit them today in Montagnola. – Also, we'll take the car that has been offered to us, since this time Mrs. Hesse spoke to me about it! – ...

ROMAIN ROLLAND'S DIARY

(September 17, 1933) – Visited Hermann Hesse in his charming house in Montagnola on the ridge of the Golden Hill above the vineyards and chestnut trees. He had us picked up in a friend's car. He awaits us with his wife and sister in front of his house. The misfortunes of our time have not marked his face which appears much fresher, calmer, and younger than the last time I saw him (two years ago on the eve of his remarriage). He complains only about his eyes which cause him some concern. Indiscreetly I perceive more anxiety on his wife's face. She is a brunette with intelligent and attractive features. As far as the sister is concerned, she is a kind, stocky old lady who doesn't speak, but who listens with an assenting smile. – Hesse alludes only briefly at the beginning of our conversation to the afflictions caused by the events in Germany and the passage of emigrants in the Tessin. – But throughout the balance of the conversation, Hesse reveals that he is quite detached and ill-informed – (he avoids the reality of events that threaten to destroy his fragile mental equilibrium). He readily satisfies himself with the idea that the true German culture will remain safeguarded from the torrent. And he loves to cite the example of a friend, a musicologist who at this very moment is preoccupied with his research in folklore. – Also, in his innermost being Hesse feels utter contempt for *Führers* – especially Hitler, whom he considers mediocre, but well attuned to the mediocre German sensitivity and therefore chosen by those who manage the whole business. But Hesse declares he is completely detached from his fatherland (which, he adds, he wouldn't have said, nor felt, during the war of 1914). – However, he didn't have to suffer personally. No measures have been take against him in this respect: he continues to publish in Germany. The letters he receives from his young readers are quite similar to those he received in previous years. Undoubtedly because his public, like him, flees into art and dreams from the pressures of reality. – For a year and a half Hesse has been working, but without haste, on a utopian work whose form he is in no hurry to find. It would depict an elite that is the lord of the key – of all keys – of the mind: arts, science, metaphysics, and occult powers – in future centuries or millenia. These men wouldn't even need to create works. They would possess in the form of mysterious formulas the absolute harmony of all powers of the mind united in it (music and mathematics, etc.). To put it briefly, the height of detachment. Psychoanalysis would say: the return to the centre of the maternal womb, in the nirvana of the embryo. – But Hesse will never realize it as well as in absorbing himself in it, without writing about it. Nothing impels him any more to do so. His beautiful house and his supporter have shielded him from the need to act – even with his pen. I don't think that this is good for him. – His most substantial artistic activity is his work as aquarellist. He delights in colours. And every day he adds one sheet after another to his collection of landscapes. – Last spring Hesse saw Thomas Mann who seems the most contemplative and worthiest among all the great German émigrés. This man who comes perhaps farthest – (for he was basically a great German bourgeois, most attached to the city and the fatherland, and I was harsh toward him in 1914-1915) – will probably have the courage to go furthest along the path of abandoning his former prejudices and convictions. But he will do so only after long and private struggles with his conscience and meditation. When he is strengthened in his convictions, it's likely that his daily life will conform to them, whatever risks it may involve. – With regard to Gerhart Hauptmann who, it is said, has just established his alliance with today's rulers by writing a hymn to Horst Wessel – as a result Hauptmann is celebrated and his plays are staged. Hesse claps his hands and laughingly says: "Bravo". As far as Hesse is concerned, Hauptmann is essentially stupid with some strokes of genius as a writer. He doesn't contradict himself. In his versatility Hauptmann is true to himself. – ...

ROMAIN ROLLAND TO MADELEINE ROLLAND

Park Hotel, Lugano,
Monday, September 18, 1933.

– ... Yesterday we saw Hermann Hesse again in his beautiful house in Montagnola. He was with his wife and his sister

– an elderly, stout woman. Except for a few comments made at the beginning on the problems resulting from events in Germany, Hesse didn't seem to us to suffer in the least – neither materially nor mentally. On the material side no measures have been taken against him, and he continues to be published in Germany. As to his mental well-being, Hesse's tranquillity, his healthy colour and his youthful look make you conscious of it. At the top of his promontory on the Golden Hill he doesn't risk being overwhelmed. He certainly expresses complete contempt for all *Führers* (and particularly for Hitler, whom he regards as intelligent, but used like an instrument attuned to the average opinion in Germany). However Hesse admits that he is now completely detached from Germany and its destiny. He had never felt like this during the war (and he says so). He has no fatherland. He is only interested in universal and timeless spiritual values, and he is confident that they will remain intact under the passing currents. Hesse doesn't exert himself. For a year and a half he has been working on a utopian work, dreaming of an imaginary élite (perhaps he believes in it) that will come about in some centuries (or millennia). In short, he escapes from the present – rather conveniently – in his beautiful home that is well-built, well-lighted, and for the winter well-heated – situated above woods and meadows. He is in no rush to write. His leisure is taken up mostly by his water-colours. He does some every day – even though his eyes give him some trouble.

Sometime this year he saw Thomas Mann who seems among the prominent émigrés the one who realizes most acutely the calamities of our time and his duty. Yet Thomas Mann was just the one who had to accomplish most to overcome the past, for he was deeply rooted in the old bourgeoisie. – Of Hauptmann, who has just publicly allied himself with the Nazis by writing an ode to Horst Wessel (!), Hesse says that he is an absolute fool – with the strokes of a writer's genius.

1936

HERMANN HESSE TO ROMAIN ROLLAND

Montagnola, January 26, 1936.

Dear and honoured Romain Rolland,

You will be seventy years old! Although these are not times for celebrating, I must nevertheless greet you on this day and assure you of my steadfast affection and respect. Since our first meeting in the Autumn of 1914, you belong for me to the few authors of our time whom I revere because of their purity and their humanity as examples and older brothers.

The experiences which we met with then during the World War are all repeating themselves again today. And the great tempation repeats itself also once again: to doubt generally the value of the Spirit and the Word. That I can resist this temptation even today, though I go through some very horrible experiences, is largely due to you.

Best wishes,

Gratefully yours,

Hermann Hesse

ROMAIN ROLLAND TO HERMANN HESSE

Villeneuve, January 31, 1936.

Dear Friend,

How touched I am that you have thought of writing me on the occasion of my seventieth birthday. You are one of my very rare brothers in art and in sentiment whom I love and respect. Your friendship makes me happy indeed.

We – you and I – are two recluses. But in my retreat I let all the world's gusts affect me; and I often long for the tranquillity of your hermitage. I haven't lived the dream of my life, but its destiny. And it always forced new struggles on me whenever I thought of rest. But never rest! – Yet I will earn it in the end! I have paid for it.

For those blessed times when we will only sleep, sleep forever, I am dreaming not of a willow weeping for my sleep – like Musset – but of an olive tree in the sun. Throughout my life I have always been nostalgic for the Italy I knew when I was twenty.

Affectionately,
Your old friend,

Romain Rolland

HERMANN HESSE TO ROMAIN ROLLAND

Dear Friend,

Your greetings delighted me.

I have read one of your new books.[1] I have just begun reading the second – that's how I celebrate your seventieth birthday. I love the vigour and vivacity of your books!

My life in Montagnola isn't quite as tranquil as it appears to you. For instance, at the present time I am again the target of persistent persecution by the press including calumny, falsified biographical data, etc. Indeed, I find myself, as usual, between two hostile fronts and am attacked from both sides. This time it's the Nazis in Germany, or rather some of my colleagues there, and at the same time the German emigrants on whose behalf I have done a lot of work in the past three years and for whom I have made great sacrifices. The world hasn't changed. It has always been at war since the days we got acquainted.

Let us hope that death will grant us one day the truly great peace for which we yearn at times. My younger brother, a poor little employee in a factory, away from his wife and children, recently committed suicide. With some envy I saw him in his grave, but then I returned to my activities, to the *vita activa* – of which we never know whether we are in fact its subject or its object.

My wife extends greetings to you, as well as to Mrs. Rolland, and I too sincerely greet you.

Yours,

H. Hesse

(Undated letter. Postmark: Montagnola. February 5, 1936)

---

[1] Undoubtedly the last volumes of *The Enchanted Soul* in German.

1938

HERMANN HESSE TO ROMAIN ROLLAND

Montagnola, March 1938.

Dear Romain Rolland,

For some years now we have left one another in peace, and only reluctantly do I disturb you today. But I appeal to you with a request, and it's an important one indeed. It concerns two persons in Russia who – mistakenly and completely innocently – have come under suspicion and are being persecuted. I beseech you to please forward a letter directly to Stalin to put in a word for these two persons. They are both members of the ingelligentsia and both have rendered service to freedom and Russia.

These are briefly the data concerning these persons:

The Swabian writer Dr. Karl Schmuckle was for several years in Moscow the editor of *Internationale Literatur.* In the past he used to fight in Germany as a Spartacist. He has been working for many years in Russia. He fell into disgrace for some unknown reason and has been imprisoned somewhere in the USSR. He is a man of integrity and of noble character. His wife, Dr. Anna Berfeld, a doctor, fears she will experience the same fate. Both are very much afraid for their little boy Micha, who is eight years old. He would be alone if his mother were arrested and would certainly be forever lost to his parents.

The other person on whose behalf I also ask you to intercede is a lady. Dr. Valy Adler, a specialist in economics, is the daughter of the famous psychologist Alfred Adler (individual psychology). Dr. Adler was formerly employed by the Russian Board of Trade in Berlin, and being always loyal, she later worked for the Publishers of the Foreign Workers in Moscow. She disappeared a year ago and it isn't known why or where she was arrested.

Some time before his death, Mazaryk intervened on her behalf, but he didn't receive an answer. It's assumed that Valy Adler incurred suspicion because she had married a Hungarian named Sas, who certainly tolerated in his factory some Trotskyites, that is to say he didn't denounce them, and undoubtedly he was a friend of Bela Kun. This young woman's family hasn't had any news from her for a year and has never been able to learn what she has been accused of. I add that until very recently she held an Austrian passport.

Dear Romain Rolland, whether it will serve a useful purpose or not, please fulfil my request: intercede with Stalin on behalf of Karl Schmuckle and of his wife, as well as on behalf of Valy Adler.

As far as I am personally concerned, I receive from Germany, as you can imagine, only few signs of friendship. But it isn't worth talking about.

My wife and I greet you both.

Faithfully yours,

Hermann Hesse

(Postmark: 3.III.38)

ROMAIN ROLLAND TO HERMANN HESSE

Villeneuve (Vaud),
Villa Olga,
March 5, 1938.

Dear Friend,

This is my present situation: Eight months ago a doctor friend of mine* in Leningrad, whom I have known for twenty years, was imprisoned without any explanation and no news has been received from him since then. Passionately I have done everything I could do for him; I have written to all leaders (twice to Stalin), to all who could know and help him – and I never received even a single word in response in those eight months.

It's the same with all the letters I've written for the past two years for the many others whom I knew who have been arrested or disappeared – Silence.

Can you imagine that I would receive an answer for people whom I don't know personally?

While Gorki was alive I could do much through his mediation. – Now, nothing.

The "philosophers" (as they used to say in Jean-Jacques' days) are no longer important among the masters who are in power.

I greet you affectionately. Please extend my kindest regards to Mrs. Hesse and greetings from my wife.

Sincerely yours,

Romain Rolland

P.S. – I'm leaving Switzerland this summer to take up residence in France – in my province, in Vézelay (Yonne). Nevertheless I'll return for the winter months every year to Villeneuve, where my lease binds me until 1940. However, as of this summer, my residence will be in France.

---

* Professor Oscar Hartoch, the brother of Elsa Hartoch, a friend of Romain Rolland since World War I.

HERMANN HESSE TO ROMAIN ROLLAND

March, 1938

Dear and honoured Friend,

You answered me so quickly and with such kindness that I must thank you very much. My request to you to intervene on behalf of these persons in Russia wasn't easy. I didn't believe that it would bring results and I know how much you are in demand. But these people's lives were endangered. They were very warmly recommended to me by very good friends, and so I had to do everything I could within my power.

The news that you'll soon leave Switzerland distresses me. Although we haven't seen each other often, I nevertheless always knew that you were there on the shore of Lake Geneva, in the same country, almost my neighbour, and that I could always expect to see you again. Now conversations, exchanges of opinions, and advice no longer seem as desirable as recognizing again a friendly look in human eyes, the presence of something fraternal while the world becomes increasingly noisy, mechanized and inhuman.

Please accept as a token of my unchanged affection this little book of mine which undoubtedly you don't know yet.*

Cordial greetings to both of you from my wife and myself.

Yours

Hermann Hesse

---

* *Stunden im Garten* (Hours in the Garden.)

ROMAIN ROLLAND TO HERMANN HESSE

Villeneuve, April 1, 1938.

Dear Friend,

What a precious little book your *Stunden im Garten* is! And how touched I am that you sent it to me! We have you alive and present with us, you and your garden which form one entity. You will no longer leave us. In the future you will still be found there on the Golden Hill. Affectionately I greet the gardener-poet.

Your admirer and friend,

Romain Rolland

Please remember me to your wife and kind regards from my wife to the beautiful gardener!

P.S. At the end of May we leave for Vézelay (via Avalon – some old names of the oldest part of France). – But I believe I already told you that I won't leave Switzerland permanently. My lease for the Villa Olga doesn't expire until the summer of 1940. We'll come back here for the winter months.

1940

ROMAIN ROLLAND TO HERMANN HESSE

(Postcard)

Switzerland
Herrn Hermann Hesse
Montagnola, Lugano
(Tessin).

Vezelay (Yonne),
14 grande rue,
August 4, 1940.

Dear Friend,

From Vézelay's blessed hill, which we haven't left, I send you on the Golden Hill affectionate and nostalgic greetings. May they make you appreciate even more lovingly the radiant and free peace of the air you breathe. I enjoy it through you.

Affectionately,

R.

My (poor) health persists – neither more nor less. The work too. That's the best.

(On the card: *Censor's stamp:*
Return to Sender)

Appendices

BEGINNING OF THE INTRODUCTION TO **KRIEG UND FRIEDEN*** *A COLLECTION OF ARTICLES BY HERMANN HESSE*** *Dedicated to the Memory of My Dear Romain Rolland*

For the present writer, assembling the elements of this book was not a pleasant task – one of those that bring to mind pleasant memories and beloved images. On the contrary, each article revived the bitter memory of times of suffering, of struggles, of isolation, of hostility, and of misunderstanding, when ideals and pleasant habits had to be bitterly neglected. That's why I opposed these shadows, which are today more hateful and more real than ever, with something beautiful and radiant – the figure of the noble, great friend to whom this book is dedicated, and with whom the only element of lasting beauty which these battles and miseries once brought me, is linked.

I have forgotten much of those agonizing days of the year 1914 when the first of these articles *(O Freunde, nicht diese Töne!)* was written. But I have not forgotten the day I received Romain Rolland's letter which was the only sympathetic reaction to my article and which at the same time announced that he sent me his book.

I had a fellow traveller, a spiritual brother, who as I, had felt the outrageous madness of the war and of the psychosis of war and had revolted against it. And this wasn't just any man. This was a man in whom I greatly appreciated the author of the first volumes of *Jean-Christophe* (I didn't know anything else by him at the time) and who was quite superior to me in education and political knowledge. We remained friends until he died. We lived too far from each other and we had cultural habits and patterns of thinking that were too different for me to become one of his followers and learn much from him in politics. But that wasn't what mattered! I had begun on my political road very late, as a man of forty, aroused and disturbed by the frightening reality of the war, greatly surprised by the ease with which my former colleagues and friends put themselves at Moloch's disposal. I had also already experienced the first losses of friends, the first attacks, threats, and insults which, in this period of so-called grandeur, some men brought into line do not fail to speak out against someone who marches alone. Could I hold out, not succumb to the conflict which turned into hell my life that until that time had been rather happy and crowned with successes that surpassed my merits? It was good, therefore, it was my salvation and good fortune, to know that a man who came from the side of the "enemy", from the French side, had expressed the same conscientious objection against the demands of submission and participation in the orgies of hatred and morbid nationalism. Neither during the war years, nor later, did I have any political discussions with Rolland, and yet I do not know if without his neighbourliness and company I could have borne up through those years. This had to be remembered here. – ...

---

* *War and Peace*

** Published by the Fretz and Wasmuth Verlag, Zürich, 1946, and by the Suhrkamp Verlag, Frankfurt/Main, 1949.

HERMANN HESSE: ON ROMAIN ROLLAND (1948)

We know what Leo Tolstoy meant for the development of the very young Romain Rolland. The letter of the youth to the old man was taken seriously and answered. Seriously and lovingly the famous man replied to the disciple's questions. In a manner that was both paternal and fraternal, he prevailed agains the impulsiveness of the anguished youth. Thus the venerable old man accomplished a sacred and magic act, the act of vocation. On several occasions in the course of his rich life, Rolland remembered this vocation and reiterated this appeal by the elder who is steadfast to the younger questers whenever he believed them of good will. Romain Rolland served both his own generation and the two succeeding ones as one who inspired and stimulated and called forth; and he was a counsellor, comrade in the struggle, and supporter during periods of opposition. Rolland guarded a flame that has not been extinguished – not even in Germany, where during the time of terror his forbidden books strengthened the opinion and roused the conscience of the faithful ones, and sustained their courage. Even today I receive from Germany reminders of Romain Rolland. I am questioned about my personal recollections of him and am asked for books by Rolland.

One finds scattered throughout the world very many faithful and pious people outside the Churches and denominations – men of good will. They are profoundly alarmed by the decline of humanism and the gradual degeneration of peace and trust in mankind throughout the world. For these good people there are no priests and no religious consolations. But those who cry out in the wilderness, saints, and martyrs do exist for them too. Romain Rolland was one of them, just like Leo Tolstoy who had inspired and stimulated him, and Mahatma Gandhi, his comrade and friend. They died, these three great consolers. Yet they live on in a thousand hearts. And they help thousands to remain faithful and to defy with their light this world which is passive and irrational.

ALBRECHT GOES: HERMANN HESSE AND ROMAIN ROLLAND*

Beethoven's entreaty – rising as the *vox humana* in the Ninth Symphony at the very moment when all cataclysms of anguish have been swept away and all expectations are directed towards the Exaltation of Joy, this mighty *"O Freunde, nicht diese Töne!"* – stands at the beginning of this beautiful, spiritual bond between Hermann Hesse and Romain Rolland whose correspondence is presented here. Shortly after World War I Hermann Hesse had published under the title of "O Freunde, nicht diese Töne!" a simple and earnest text – an exhortation to the intellectuals of all nations that contained *one* request: even though insanity already runs rampant, the intellectuals at least should maintain above the barbed wire their spiritual purity, their breadth of vision, and the consciousness of a last unity. This warning was softly spoken – *sotto voce*, so to speak – by reason and love. But it immediately aroused the wrath of the nationalists of many countries and especially that of Hesse's fellow-Germans. With the letters of insult there came only *one* fraternal acclamation, an expression of gratitude and joy: Romain Rolland's acclaim. Thus the bond was created. Subsequently the two men mutually strengthened this spiritual comradeship, this friendship. The word friendship is truly justified for this communion of care and love that spanned more than twenty-five years, but included some considerable interruptions which are, however, not surprising among men who have a rich, personal world.

Such a publication transmits something of the attraction of old frescoes. Very little of it becomes visible, but a lot can be imagined. Even when the two partners don't fully reveal themselves, the profiles of their respective individuality become clear. Hesse's shy, hermit-like existence, his "Asian passivity", the courageous, anxious, difficult trials of the life of an artist – of the pure artist. And on the other hand: Romain Rolland's loving glance, Jean-Christophe's intellectually vigorous passion for life, the yearning for it, to participate in it, to become committed, to bear responsibility, to fight for an idea – all that makes Rolland, who is eleven years older than Hesse, often enough seem like the younger of the two of this fellowship. And the nobility with which differences of opinion about individual questions are dealt with in these pages becomes apparent, just like the joy which each of them experiences as he welcomes the other's work: Rolland Hesse's *Siddhartha* and Hesse Rolland's book of "The Enchanted Soul" entitled *Annette and Sylvie.* Finally, we see the respect with which the creators of the past – Goethe and Beethoven for Rolland, Mozart and Jean Paul for Hesse – are regarded and how they are associated with their own destinies as time progresses. Close by appears also the face of a contemporary, great responsible man - Mahatma Gandhi.

The penultimate letter – Rolland's expression of thanks for Hesse's peaceful and serene idyll *Stunden im Garten* bears the date April 1, 1938. But then the censors have the last word. The nations are drawn into Hitler's war and the total breakdown of everything for which these two men fought here seems to materialize. However it is important to recognize – and this is, it seems to me, the most significant aspect of this publication – that these two idealistic individuals who recognized in advance quite clearly the triumph of inhumanity, yet never resigned themselves to *one* tone – that of resignation. Romain Rolland doesn't yearn for a weeping willow on his grave, but for the olive tree in the sun. And Hesse doesn't envision anything different:

"Kann ich nicht siegen als Held,
*Will ich doch fallen als Streiter."***

Light through wandering clouds: how it directs our attention to the unsettled spectacle of our time! With dismay we contemplate the past and with alarm we behold the present.

But what really matters, and we know it well, is a watchful eye to safeguard the future.

Albrecht Goes

Gebersheim/Württemberg,
January, 1954.

---

* Introduction in Hermann Hesse/Romain Rolland *Briefe,* Fretz and Wasmuth, Zurich, 1954.

** "Can't I triumph as hero, let me die a fighter".

Index of Names

Index of works by Hesse and Rolland

HESSE

ROLLAND